ARISE TO PEACE

For Laura —
May this encourage
you & bring you peace♡
Julie Coleman

Arise to Peace
Daily Devotional

General Editor
Julie Zine Coleman

Right to the Heart

Bold Vision Books
PO Box 2011
Friendswood, Texas 77549

ISBN 9781946708-57-1
Library of Congress Control Number 2021933276

Table of Contents

Foreword

A COVID-filled sneeze sprays the air and you cover your nose, trying not to breathe. As the cloud spreads around you, you make a break for it, plowing into a swirl of murder hornets. You swat at them as you pivot, skidding your tennis shoes as you plow head-on into a riot of screaming people waving signs plastered with your face. You pull up your bandana and look for a place to hide, but too late, they've spotted you, and they've set off a shriek that would wake the dead.

Your heart skips a beat, and you stir in your bed. In that moment, relief sweeps over you.

What you experienced was only a nightmare. Thank goodness. You sit up to turn off your alarm and stare directly into the face of a TV commentator who says, "Welcome to today."

Images flash across the screen and your nightmare replays with pandemics, riots, murder hornets, and enough political spin to make you dizzy. This day is going to be anything but peaceful, right?

But wait. Jesus said in John 16:33, "I have told you these things, so that in me you may have peace. In this world you will have trouble. But take heart! I have overcome the world."

What was Jesus really saying? "Figure out the right prayer to pray and I'll snap my fingers and make all your troubles disappear?"

I think Jesus was saying we can have His peace, even in troubled times.

Jesus is all-powerful, but He seems to be up to a miracle that's a little out of our perspective. I think He's using the cover of darkness to allow His peace to shine in and through us, so that we can light the way for others so that they too can meet him and have the peace that passes understanding.

Imagine how the disciples felt when they realized Jesus was leaving them again, this time to return to heaven. He told them, "I am leaving you with a gift—peace of mind and heart. And the peace I give is a gift the world cannot give. So don't be troubled or afraid" (John 14: 27 NIV).

This word is also for us. It's time to claim our gift of peace so we can fill the lamp of our lives with more of His presence.

I'm glad you've landed with your nose in this book, because my friends are going to encourage you with their testimonies of how they found God's peace in the most unlikely places.

May their stories help you find the peace that passes understanding, no matter the news of the day.

~Linda Evans Shepherd; Author of *Praying Through Every Emotion* and President of Right to the Heart Ministries and founder of the Arise Esther Movement

Introduction
Julie Zine Coleman

Shalom!

In biblical times, this greeting wished a wholeness for the other person's satisfaction in life and rest. We might first think of peace as an absence of war. But in biblical times, the idea of shalom was not just about nations. It included harmony between persons or families or nations. It could also communicate safety or even prosperity.

There's one more aspect of *shalom* that may surprise you: God's peace has little to do with our circumstances. And much more to do with our hearts.

Isaiah called Jesus the Messiah the "Prince of Peace." He came to remove the obstacle of sin that kept us from a relationship with God. He suffered our punishment and paid our debt in full, so we could be at peace with Him. The members of the Advanced Writers and Speakers Association have come together to create this set of daily devotionals to point you to the provider and reason for our peace.

Peace is not something we can conjure up within ourselves. It is a by-product of a relationship with God. The better we know Him, the more His peace will rule our hearts. In his second epistle, Peter prayed, "May grace and peace be multiplied to you through the knowledge of God and of Jesus our Lord" (2 Peter 1:2 CSB). A growing knowledge of God is key to our maintaining peace.

We would like to recommend you go beyond a passive reading each day. Try the following methods to enhance your time with the Lord and in His Word.

- Always begin with prayer. If you are a believer, the Holy Spirit resides in you to guide, teach, and inspire you in your walk with Him. Ask Him to use this time to stimulate spiritual growth in you, transforming you into the image of Christ.

- Open your Bible. Read not only the verse for the day, but the context around it. What comes before and after the verse? How does this verse fit within the whole? You will find compelling stories in each day's Arise Daily to Peace selection, but the real power is in the Word of God. Giving more than a cursory read is an opportunity to find valuable truth that will impact your understanding.

- Look for the main idea. What is the main truth the author is trying to express? What would you like to remember from today's reading that is relevant to you today?

- Take a few minutes to journal your thoughts. Have you experienced what the author is talking about? What thought or sentence really spoke to your heart? Why did you need to see this article?

- Spend time dwelling in God's presence. Ask Him questions that occurred to you in your study. Pray over the Scripture. Be still and allow Him to direct your thoughts. Praise Him for who He is and express your love and gratitude for all He means to you. Share your concerns for the day and beyond.

As you invest time in Him, God will draw you closer. He wants to meet with you and will reward your efforts. And may the resulting peace of God, which surpasses all comprehension, guard your heart and mind in Christ Jesus (Philippians 4:7).

~Julie Zine Coleman, General Editor

Day 1

Living in the Moment

Babbie Mason

"None of this fazes us because Jesus loves us. I'm
absolutely convinced that nothing—nothing living or
dead, angelic or demonic, today or tomorrow, high or
low, thinkable or unthinkable—absolutely nothing can
get between us and God's love because of the way that
Jesus our Master has embraced us"

(Romans 8:38-39 THE MESSAGE).

Everyone knows what it feels like to be rejected. Were you rejected on the playground at school when you were a child? Maybe you've been crushed by the sting of rejection because of your skin color. Ever been told you're not good enough, not pretty enough, that you don't belong, or that you don't measure up?

Rejection cuts deep. If you were rejected as a child, the bitter taste, more than likely, remains. And if you've been rejected as an adult, you know how it feels to struggle, believing you matter, but feeling like you don't. Rejection can leave you stuck. Paralyzed in the middle of nowhere. Left alone to experience the pangs of insignificance, emptiness, and isolation.

There is Someone who will never reject you. His name is Jesus. With Jesus, you are always accepted. You are His beloved child and the object of His affections. Knowing that nothing can come between you and God's love brings heartfelt assurance, joy, peace, and purpose to life. If anyone knows the pain of rejection, Jesus does. The Prophet Isaiah reminds us in Isaiah 53:3 that Jesus was "despised and rejected." Jesus was rejected by His own people, the Jews. Worst of all, Jesus was rejected by those who were His closest friends, the disciples.

So, what must you remember today? You can find consolation today in knowing Jesus not only feels your pain, but He can heal your heart.

Start by making a choice. Obsessing over the pain of the past fixes nothing. That only causes regret. Worrying about tomorrow won't add value to your life. That only brings on more worry. Being in either of those places robs you of joy and the peace available to you right now through the Peace-Giver, Jesus Christ.

Instead of living nowhere, live now here. Live in the peace of this present moment, realizing you are deeply loved by God. You are His beloved. You are His favorite. Then bask in the deep end of His love, knowing that nothing, no thing, not even rejection, can come between you and the way Jesus our Master has embraced you. Make the bold confession today that you are the beloved of God. Determine to walk in the peace and stand on the promise that you are accepted and approved by God and nothing can ever change that!

Day 2

It is Well

Nan Corbitt Allen

"And the peace of God, which transcends all understanding, will guard your hearts and your minds in Christ Jesus."

(Philippians 4:7 NIV)

"Saved alone…"

That was the text on the telegram sent by a grieving wife to her husband, Horatio Spafford.

Spafford was a successful lawyer in the mid-1800's in Chicago.

During the great Chicago fire of 1871, Spafford had lost a lot of property. The stress of that trouble prompted Horatio and his family to take a vacation in Europe. On the November 1873 departure date, Horatio was detained with business matters, but he sent his wife and four daughters on ahead. En route, their ship, the S.S. Ville du Havre, collided with an English vessel. It sank in a matter of minutes. Mrs. Spafford survived, but all four girls were lost at sea.

"Saved alone."

Spafford immediately set out to meet his despondent wife in England. As his ship approached the place where the S. S. Ville du Havre had sunk, Horatio asked the captain to stop while he wrote the lyrics to his now-beloved song.

"When peace, like a river, attendeth my way,

When sorrows like sea billows roll;

Whatever my lot, Thou hast taught me to say,

'It is well, it is well with my soul.'"

Peace. It is probably humanity's greatest pursuit. Satan can use that desire as a tool in his deception—and whispers promises of peace into the ears of those looking for a quick path out of conflict.

The meaning of "peace," in a spiritual sense, is far deeper than mere avoidance of conflict. But it's hard to explain, because, as Paul the Apostle said in Philippians 4:7, it "transcends all understanding" (NASB). To understand spiritual peace, one needs to experience it.

"You will keep in perfect peace those whose minds are steadfast, because they trust in you" (Isaiah 26:3 NIV). Note the sequence: trust comes before the perfect peace. It is knowing that what God has done before, He can do again.

Even before His death and resurrection, Jesus talked about peace, then qualified it after the Passover meal to His disciples.

"Peace I leave with you; my peace I give you. I do not give to you as the world gives." (John 14:27a NIV). Was this a new peace? Before, peace had been linked to a sense of well-being and fulfillment, lacking nothing essential. Was Jesus implying that this was a peace never experienced?

Later on in the speech, Jesus said, "I have told you these things, so that in me you may have peace. In this world you will have trouble. But take heart! I have overcome the world" (John 16:33 NIV).

Later that evening, Jesus went out to the garden to pray and was arrested there. Before another day had passed, he suffered a violent execution. How could peace be found in such a situation?

Paul equates peace with being in harmony with God through a right standing through faith in His Son. "Therefore, since we have been justified through faith, we have peace with God through our Lord Jesus Christ, through whom we have gained access by faith into this grace in which we now stand" (Romans 5:1-2 NIV).

This is true peace, not as the world gives, but that which passes human understanding. We can have an enduring harmony with God in the middle of life's tragedies and heartache.

Day 3

When Darkness Threatens

Lucinda Secrest McDowell

"Confuse them, Lord, and frustrate their plans, for I see
violence and conflict in the city... Everything is falling
apart; threats and cheating are rampant in the streets ...
Morning, noon, and night I cry out in my distress, and
the Lord hears my voice ... But you, O God, will send
the wicked down to the pit of destruction."

(Psalm 55.9, 11, 17, 23 NLT)

I walked into the living room just in time to catch the evening
news. As the broadcaster spoke, I gasped and burst into tears. Not
one, but two violent shootings had killed thirty-one innocent people in El Paso and Dayton in less than twenty-four hours!

How could this be?

Today, as I write, on the 217th day of 2019, there have already been
255 mass shootings in the United States. That's more than one for
each day. Panic, not peace, fills my heart.

I don't want to hear the news anymore; I just want to hide and
hope it will all go away. But Jesus called me to live in the world,
even when it is a frightening, dark place. We believers are to shine
as lights into this encroaching darkness.

I don't feel very bright. The whole country is arguing about who is to blame, why this violence keeps happening, complaining that prayer is not enough! I know we need to *both* pray and act. I often turn to David's psalms of lament, like Psalm 55.

I "cry out in distress" asking God to "confuse them, Lord, and frustrate their plans." Those evil plans for random killing, for violence and conflict. Not just in cities, but in suburbs and countryside. No region of our country has been spared this evil.

We feel many emotions when breaking news reveals yet another act of violence against helpless, ordinary people. Anger. Fear. Incredulity. Shock. Sadness. Compassion. Horror. Anxiety.

How do we as Christ followers respond?

First, we *lament*. We weep and collapse in sorrow. We acknowledge all the feelings, knowing that burying them makes it worse. Then we move beyond, as the psalmist did, and *look* to God by crying out to Him in prayer and entreaty. Yet again we can be assured that "the Lord hears my voice." He will bring a peace to my soul that the world cannot give.

But how do we then keep going? We choose to *live*. Yes, even when twenty-two people were just murdered at Walmart while shopping for back-to-school supplies. That day, as a personal act of refusing to live in fear, I deliberately shopped at Walmart and made a point of greeting everyone I saw. Of course, there are far more pro-active ways to live and honor their memory. Each of us must decide how to encourage change, both in individuals and in society.

When such horrific tragedy occurs, we *lament*, we *look* to God, we *live* intentionally, and then we do perhaps the hardest thing of all—we *leave* our concerns in the hands of powerful God Almighty. Do we trust Him enough to be the ultimate judge and jury for the wicked?

King David knew this to be the final answer, as he entrusted the Lord to *"send the wicked down to the pit of destruction"* (Psalm 53:23 NLT).

I cannot even imagine how I would feel if it were my loved ones targeted by bullets at a concert, school, theatre, shopping mall, or even while worshipping in a church. But I believe I must leave all my fears, my anger, and my need for justice in the hands of the Creator and Sustainer of the universe.

Instead of falling to pieces when the world is torn apart, I can choose to live as a peacemaker.

May God our Refuge shine brightest in our darkness and bring hope and healing to our hurting world. And may He use me, His servant, to lead the way.

Day 4

Instrument of Peace

Candy Arrington

"Don't worry about anything, but pray about everything. With thankful hearts offer up your prayers and
requests to God. Then, because you belong to Christ
Jesus, God will bless you with peace that no one can
completely understand. And this peace will control the
way you think and feel."

(Philippians 4:6-7 CEV)

"I'm so glad it's you!" exclaimed a beautiful young woman as she
took the seat next me on the plane. I looked up from my book, sur-
prised, half expecting to see a familiar face, but she was a stranger.

"You see," she continued, as if we were old friends, "I was so afraid
I would be stuck beside some huge guy who took up his seat and
part of mine for the whole flight. I would have been miserable!"

As we prepared for takeoff, my husband, who was seated several
rows in front of me with our children, came back to check on me
and say, "I love you." Again, the young woman turned to me and
said, "How sweet. Your husband must love you very much."

As she continued to talk, I put the book I was reading in the seat pocket in front of me. Through the Holy Spirit's prompting, I knew this woman needed my time and full attention.

I listened as she poured out her story—her abandonment at age two by a drug and alcohol abusing mother, her denial of and struggles with Multiple Sclerosis, and her fears regarding being frequently left alone with her two children while her husband traveled on business. She had missed an earlier flight because she clung to her sons, fearful that something would happen to them, or her, during their separation.

Although a Christian, she was living in bondage to her fears. I asked if I could share some Scripture with her, and when I returned from retrieving my Bible from an overhead bin, she said, "Now I understand why I missed my flight. God put me beside you so you could help me with my fear!"

I turned to Philippians 4:6-7 and read it to her, stressing that the blessing of surrendering fears and anxious thoughts to God brings peace. Verses in Psalms provided comfort in dealing with the depression she experiences due to health problems. I shared Philippians 4:13 and encouraged her to ask God for the strength and courage to overcome her fear of needles and give herself the injections necessary for her MS.

I suggested she make Bible study a part of her daily routine, in addition to church attendance, explaining that just as we physically eat more than once a week, we need daily spiritual nourishment. She pulled paper and pen from her purse and made notes. As the plane made its descent, we exchanged names and email addresses, squeezed hands, and eyes glistening with tears, went our separate ways.

Often, God places those in our path who are struggling and in turmoil. With perception and willingness, each of us can become an instrument of peace. So, the next time you're annoyed by a delay, or you experience an interruption to your routine, look closely to see if God is positioning you to minister peace to one of His hurting children.

Day 5

Giving Control to God

Kristine Brown

"They will have no fear of bad news; their hearts are
steadfast, trusting in the Lord."

(Psalm 112:7 NIV)

I watched him climb the three-foot retaining wall at the park, his
legs pushing his stocky frame upward. As he stood on the make-
shift balance beam, arms stretched out wide, my mom instincts
kicked into high gear. I rushed to hold my five-year-old's hand,
helping him walk safely to the end of the wall.

I remember hearing my husband chuckle as I rushed off to offer unneeded support. "The wall's only three feet high," he said.
"What's the worst that could happen?" He knew this wasn't the
only time I had unnecessarily run to my son's rescue.

I adored my God-given calling to be a mom. Loving my son, caring
for him, and protecting him was my greatest joy. But in my zeal
to keep him safe, was I being too controlling? My husband knew
something I had yet to learn. If I didn't let him try on his own, he
wouldn't know how to pick himself up after a fall. I needed to let
go.

Parenting wasn't the only place I craved control. Whether it was controlling my circumstances, plans, or other people, it was easy for me to excuse away my controlling habits. I'm tempted to say, "That's just who I am. A go-getter. An organizer. Someone who takes charge." But there was much more behind my inability to let go.

Control is first revealed in Scripture in Genesis chapter three, when Eve and Adam faced consequences for eating the forbidden fruit. God spoke to Eve and said, "And you will desire to control your husband..." (Genesis 3:16 NIV).

Could it be that the struggle with our need to control began when sin entered the world? One thing is certain. When I remove the mask of control, I reveal insecurities I'd rather not see. Things like fear, worry, and the desire to feel needed come to mind, and these things are not of God.

I'm guilty of trying to prevent bad news from happening. I'd rather formulate a grand escape plan than watch my son fall to the ground and scrape his knee. Only when nothing else works do I turn to God, instead of making Him my first choice.

Things won't always be easy, but we can walk through anything with assurance that God is with us, even when we fall. The verse above gives us hope today. We do not have to let fear or worry drive us to control any situation. We can turn our hearts toward God and trust the outcome to Him.

I may have prevented a scraped knee or twisted ankle all those years ago, but now that my child's a young adult, the walls of life are higher. And the risks are greater. With every decision he makes, thoughts of that day at the wall come flooding back. But instead of rushing to hold his hand this time, I see God sitting there, a safe distance away, just watching. My job is to stand back and pray this simple prayer:

Lord, as I face the day's challenges, You will be my first choice instead of my last resort. In Jesus' name, Amen.

If you're struggling to release control today, this life-changing prayer will help you change your perspective. Let's pray these words every time we desire to take control.

Remembering to give our problems to God first will replace fear, worry, and insecurity and replace them with trust, peace, and rest. May we keep our hearts focused on our Heavenly Father today. He is our first and best choice.

Day 6

Be Still

Jill Savage

"Surely I have calmed and quieted my soul"

(Psalm 131:2a AMP)

I sat in the counselor's office, eyes so swollen from an hour of crying they were barely slits in my face. "Jill, I have a homework assignment for you," he said.

"Ok," I responded, willing to do anything to get my life and my marriage put back together.

"I want you to sit for twenty minutes a day."

"And do what?" I asked.

"Be still," he said. "Focus on just breathing in and breathing out."

Exasperated, I said, "That seems like a waste of 20 minutes. I'm a git-it-done girl."

"I know," he responded. "It's time for you to be a 'quiet-your-soul' kind of girl." This kind of assignment messed with my Type A driven personality. But I listened and tried it for the week between my appointments.

Day one, I barely made it five minutes. I squirmed, assembled my grocery list in my head, and watched the clock. But I had committed to do it for a week, so I tried again. This time I made it ten minutes. I focused on my breathing. Day three I fell asleep. Sitting in my recliner. In the middle of the day. This girl, who can't sleep unless she's laying down in a dark room, slept. I woke up about twenty minutes later with the most incredible sense of peace. The Bible describes this as a "peace that passes all understanding."

My chaotic circumstances were creating a chaotic soul. That day I experienced "it is not well with my circumstances, but it is well with my soul." I knew that whether or not my husband returned, I would be okay. I knew God was with me.

"For God alone, O my soul, wait in silence, for my hope is from him"

(Psalm 62:5).

You'll be tempted to grasp at every straw you see. You'll be tempted to do, do, and do some more to change your reality. Instead, be still. Be a seeker of internal peace. God stills your soul, clears your head, and gives you the peace you're looking for.

When fear creeps in, speak the name of Jesus. Ask God for what you need. Pray against distraction. Pray for wisdom, patience, and the ability to respond rather than react to any situation. Pray as you drive, as you walk, as you get ready in the morning. You don't have to stop, fold your hands, and bow your head. Just talk to God throughout the day as you would a friend who is right beside you.

Adapted from *Your Next Steps: What to Do When Your Spouse is Unfaithful* by Jill Savage. Copyright 2017.

Day 7

Amidst the Chaos

Natalie Ford

"But hope that is seen is no hope at all. Who hopes for
what they already have? But if we hope for what we do
not yet have, we wait for it patiently. In the same way,
the Spirit helps us in our weakness. We do not know
what we ought to pray for, but the Spirit himself inter-
cedes for us through wordless groans."

(Romans 8:24-26 NIV)

When I opened the door to our home and stepped inside, I gasped
at the sight. Clothes covered every inch of the living room. Socks
littered the newly vacuumed floor I'd left that morning. Belts were
hanging from the ceiling fan, and camping supplies were strewn all
about. I raced for the phone to call 911. I couldn't believe it!

"God, no! How could someone break into our home now?" As I
reached for the phone, I heard music playing in the back room. I
slowly crept toward the doorway and found my husband Michael
flinging clothes out of drawers and tossing them across the floor.
He had emptied every drawer, every closet, and every cabinet looking for some tool he had lost. Overwhelmed at what was happening, I cried, "What are you doing?"

Surely he had some reason for this insanity! Now let me tell you, in moments like these, remembering that God works all things for the good of those who love Him was not my first thought. In that moment, I became unglued. With a crimson face, I shouted words I could never take back.

Michael was diagnosed with mental illness, yet I was the one shouting like a maniac. I realized in that moment that I couldn't go on living like this. Something had to change.

I didn't even know what to pray for anymore. Life was so desperate. I began crying out to God, much like the Psalmists. I yelled about how unjust my life was; I told him how angry I was that the man I loved had turned into someone I no longer recognized. I cried; I screamed, and then something changed me.

But in that dark moment, I learned that in my weakness, God truly is strong. When there seemed to be no hope, I knew God was there.

My circumstances did not change after my outburst to God, but something within me did. God was with me that afternoon in my living room and He is with me now. He gave me peace in the midst of the chaos by reminding me He was still in control and by reminding me He saw my pain.

My grandmother always says, "God not only knows where you are going, but He also knows what it is going to take to get you there." God sees what is ahead and He cares about our present. Imagine, God Himself, the Holy Spirit, is praying on our behalf. Let that sink in. The Creator of the universe is actively praying for you and for me. He loves with an everlasting love and promises to help us in our weakness. We have hope because God is on the throne and He cares about every detail of our lives. He will never leave us nor forsake us. He is our Peace and our Hope!

The Sovereignty of God is what gives me hope for tomorrow—hope that today's hurts are not in vain. They are preparations for the future. So, if you are going through your own time of suffering, draw near to God. Allow His presence to comfort you and give you peace.

Day 8

The Rocky Road to Peace

Lori Roeleveld

"And when they could not find them, they dragged Jason and some of the brothers before the city authorities, shouting, 'These men who have turned the world upside down have come here also, and Jason has received them, and they are all acting against the decrees of Caesar, saying that there is another king, Jesus.'"

(Acts 17:6-7 ESV)

Let's be frank. The road that leads to peace is often uncomfortable and unsettling. This came home to me during a meeting at work.

My job is to help families by addressing problems that have brought their dysfunctional parenting to the attention of authorities. A major university studying our outcomes was unhappy to discover that initially, our program increased parental anxiety rather than decrease it. It appeared to baffle them.

Not me. "May I explain?" I asked. They nodded.

"Many of the parents we serve are parenting in a way that serves them, not their children. When we arrive, of course, it disturbs their peace. We ask them to use safe methods of discipline, to address their substance abuse or neglected mental health, to obtain jobs and to wake up on time to get their children to school. The road to safe parenting is, of course, uncomfortable at first for them, but better for their children in the long run. It makes sense that we must first increase parental anxiety before the family can find peace."

Jesus-followers must keep this in mind, too, in our role as peacemakers. Jesus, His followers, and the leaders of the early church were most well-known for disturbing the peace, not making it. Their message was so upsetting to the status quo, they faced mobs, beatings, imprisonments, even death. In every place they preached the truth of Jesus Christ, there were some who found peace with God, but even more who had no room in their lives for another king.

Some of us seek an easy pathway to peace, but that's not the way of Christ. We want His peace, but not if that means changing our ways. We want His peace, but not if that requires us to speak hard truths to others. We want His peace, but not if that puts us at odds with our neighbors, coworkers, or culture. We want His peace, but we often want comfort and safety more.

Better to have what the apostles learned was available only by risking everything and by "turning the world upside down." They could worship in prisons, during storms, after stonings, beatings, threats of death, and complete rejection. Even when their actions put others, like Jason and his household at risk, they knew peace because they lived in obedience and faith.

Many of us wrestle with a lack of peace, but when God points the way, it looks so unsettling; we choose to trust our own understanding instead of what we can clearly see from the history of His people. If we cling to comfort, if we sit quietly when we should speak up, if we go along to get along, if we seek only calm waters, peace may elude us until we are home.

True followers of Jesus will never be at peace until they are willing to disturb it in the name of Jesus. May God give us boldness and wisdom to navigate our times; may He free us from our love of comfort, so that we will travel the rocky road that leads to peace.

Ask God today to unsettle you where you have grown too comfortable. Ask Him to show you where you've been silent, when you should speak. Schedule the hard conversation. Repent of the disobedience. Turn someone's world upside down.

It won't be easy, but only then you will find yourself, like the apostles, singing and praising God, filled with peace, even on the run in the dark.

Day 9

A Sure Way to Restore Peace

Debbie Wilson

"Peace I leave with you; my peace I give you. I do not give to you as the world gives. Do not let your hearts be troubled and do not be afraid."

(John 14:27 NIV)

I normally wouldn't call myself an idol worshiper, but an event forced me to reconsider. A series of unpleasant twists and turns in the road of life climaxed one morning when I discovered that one of my favorite French chairs was coming apart. At the sight, I came unglued.

Like lancing an infected boil, my ugly fears and confusion spewed out. This caused me to get down to business with the Lord. He cleaned out my infection by exposing some idols that had crept into my heart. He granted me the grace to say, "It all belongs to You. I don't want to lose these things, but I surrender it all to You. I love You more than all these things."

A simple prayer. But deep peace followed my surrender and soothed my jagged feelings.

By nature, I fight for and fix things I care about. If something is wrong, I jump in to make it right. Even while some circumstances may be good, if I'm not careful, I can end up in a power struggle with God.

Sometimes God allows things I can't mend, so I'll remember that I don't know best. I'm not in control. I pull out the white flag: "Lord, You are my captain, if this is Your will, I surrender."

When I get to heaven and see my life from God's perspective, I know I won't wish He'd written my story differently. I will marvel at His wisdom. I will worship. If I know this to be true in the future, why do I wrestle with letting go now?

Sometimes we think of surrender as resignation. But surrendering to God isn't about giving up. It's about lifting our concerns to God expecting He will do something better than we can imagine.

First Kings 17 tells of a widow who surrendered her last meal to the prophet Elijah. God used this woman's sacrifice to sustain Elijah, the woman, and her son for the rest of a three-and-a-half-year famine. Security comes with surrender.

When we give God our all, we become channels of His resources. If I yield most areas of my life and cling to just one, I have no peace. But when I give God everything, I have nothing left to worry about! I've found I need to re-surrender often as new substitutes for God are exposed. With each renewal comes fresh peace.

Recently my husband and I spent a weekend cleaning out the attic. I looked around my cleaned-out space and breathed in the peace that comes from order. We'd hauled off a lot of junk and former treasures, but it was worth the effort. "Lord Jesus, help me let go of things—material or immaterial—that clutter my life and steal my peace."

Has efficiency, security, your family, health, or feeling useful become an idol in your life? Why not offer them back to God and watch Him work?

Day 10

Peace Beyond Comprehension

Sheri Schofield

"The Lord gives his people strength. The Lord blesses
them with peace."

(Psalm 29:11 NLT)

BOOM! Pop-pop-pop-pop-pop!

I looked around at the Mexican pastors' wives in the courtyard outside the church. "*Peligro* (Danger)." I said. They nodded, and we all went calmly back inside the building.

I was teaching a class on children's ministries in the small town of Pena Blanca, about eight hours south of Juarez, Mexico. We were in La Linea Cartel territory, right on the border with the Sinaloa Cartel. Something was happening, but we didn't know what it was.

During the next session, my pastor spoke. We heard the machine gun fire coming closer until it was less than a block away. Pastor Jim stopped for the noise to pass, then continued. After the session, two of our interpreters took their children and left. They lived in Independencia, in Sinaloa territory, and needed to get out of town, for they were in danger if they stayed.

An hour and a half later, we finished teaching and headed back to the mission. As we pulled out into the main street, we saw Mexican state troopers everywhere. Some wore black masks and body armor and were standing behind machine guns. Our driver stopped to ask what was happening. La Linea Cartel had ambushed a state trooper patrol car and had killed three troopers. They were getting ready to go after the cartel.

I should have been shaken by the battle, but I was totally at peace. Two days later, I accompanied Pastor Jim to the church in Independencia, where he and I both taught. On the way home, we were stopped by about fifteen men armed with machine guns. They stood across the road, guns up. After identifying our vehicle as being non-cartel, they released us.

Again, I should have been afraid, but I was not. I was exactly where God had asked me to be. No, I did not feel invincible. But I knew God was with us, and that I was in the center of His will. What would happen would be His plan for me, whether it be life or death. My natural responses had been taken over by the Holy Spirit, who had given me supernatural peace.

Peace is not the absence of danger: it is the presence of God in our circumstances.

Shadrach, Meshach and Abednego shared that same peace when they stood before King Nebuchadnezzar. The king had ordered everyone to bow to his great idol. But these three Hebrew men did not. Their loyalty was to Jehovah.

Nebuchadnezzar apparently liked these three young men, for he gave them a second chance. "You must bow, or you will be thrown into the fiery furnace!" he ordered.

But the three men replied, "King Nebuchadnezzar, we do not need to defend ourselves before you in this matter. If we are thrown into the blazing furnace, the God we serve is able to deliver us from it, and he will deliver us from Your Majesty's hand. But even if he does not, we want you to know, Your Majesty, that we will not serve your gods or worship the image of gold you have set up." (Daniel 3:16-18 NIV)

In fury, Nebuchadnezzar commanded that the furnace to be heated seven times hotter, then ordered his guards to throw the men into it. God showed up with His faithful servants and walked with them in the fiery furnace and saved their lives.

When I remember this story, I understand the peace they felt through it all. Where God is present, there is no fear. He gives us peace so that we may serve Him confidently wherever He sends us.

Day 11

Grasping for Peace through Unanswered Prayer

Heidi McLaughlin

"For my thoughts are not your thoughts, neither are
your ways my ways. As the Heavens are higher than the
earth, so are my ways higher than your ways and my
thoughts than your thoughts."

(Isaiah 55:8, 9 NIV)

"Before we head out, I'm just gonna grab a cup of coffee." On
Remembrance Day 2016, those were the last words I heard from
my beloved husband Jack. I lunged into the kitchen when I heard
a crash and dropped to my knees in horror. Jack had collapsed, and
there was no pulse. I called 911. In between speaking to the first
responder and trying to perform CPR on Jack, I gasped for air and
kept shouting: "Oh God, please let him live, please let him live."
Then I heard the ambulance sirens!

Hope.

I couldn't bear to watch all the thumping and injections as the
paramedics brought back a pulse. Instead, silently, I prayed. *God,*

You can't possibly make me a widow for the second time, the pain is too much to bear. Please bring back a pulse and let Jack live. We have so many wonderful years still ahead of us. Then I heard the sound of hope, the beeping of a heartbeat.

Driving through heavy traffic in the ambulance gave me more time and opportunity to pray and beg God for Jack's life. As soon as we arrived at the hospital, I made phone calls to our children and closest friends. Through the next few hours, they arrived from all over North America. Through endless hugs and tears, we prayed. Oh, how we prayed. Friends, pastors and other family members arrived, and we formed many prayer circles to pray for God's graciousness, and power to save Jack's life. Sadly, five days later, he took his last breath.

I was a widow once again. I had to find peace.

Over the ensuing days and weeks, there was only one thing I wanted. Peace. Relentlessly, I prayed for the Prince of Peace to invade my heart and mind and to fill me with a calm spirit. I read all verses on peace in the Bible. I devoured the Psalms. Then I remembered Isaiah 55, where God clearly stated that His thoughts are higher and not like our human thoughts.

God has an upper story. God, the author of our lives, is writing a grander blueprint of our lives that will unfold in clarity when we see Him face to face. For reasons you and I will never know, God has to say "no" now and then.

God is clothed in majesty, but to our human eyes is shrouded in mystery. "Now we see things imperfectly, like puzzling reflections in a mirror, but then we will see everything with perfect clarity. All that I know now is partial and incomplete, but then I will know everything completely, just as God now knows me completely" (1 Corinthians 13:12 NLT).

Being assured of God's love and knowing He has a complete and majestic upper story slowed the beat of my anxious heart. Peace came. I slept knowing that I could trust God with His upper story, and that His love makes everything work out for good.

When our heart beats with anxiety, when we have more questions than answers, let's remember that there is a glorious upper story. Where one day we will see everything with complete clarity.

Day 12

Not Knowing the Reason

Georgia Shaffer

"Then they cried out to the LORD in their trouble, and
he delivered them from their dis-tress"

(Psalm 107:6 NIV).

I had lost my spiritual footing but did not realize it. In an emotional fog and totally confused after the diagnosis of stage IV cancer, I felt disconnected from God.

Although I was sure the answer was to spend more quiet time with God, pray harder, and read the Bible more, I could not seem to do these in any deep meaningful way. For eight months I did nothing. For me, a Type A personality, I felt like I had given up. I no longer cared about life. I had lost my purpose and focus.

"Though he slay me, yet will I hope in him"

(Job 13:15 NIV).

Some say we should never ask, "Why God?" But, when I'm being authentic with God and myself, this question frequently runs through my mind. Why did I have cancer? Why has it recurred? Why did You do this to me, God?

Not that I ever got an answer, but I did ask. I even had a few moments when I shook my fist at God and demanded a reply, *Are You mad at me? Am I being punished?* Still no answer.

Job never got an answer either. He never understood why he was suffering. Yet he trusted God.

It's hard to trust when I don't know the reason. But God still asks this of me. So I must answer the questions: Can I let go of my desire to reason things out? Am I willing to live without an answer and with the anxiety that uncertainty brings?

When I decided God is trustworthy despite how my life looks, my focus shifted from "Why, God?" to "I will trust You, regardless." With that change in focus came the peace of God and the courage to live where I was instead of where I wished to be.

John Ortberg explains that verses like Psalms 107:6 are Psalms of Disorientation—"psalms where the soul is disoriented, God is absent; darkness is winning."[1] The word "disoriented" shifted something inside of me. *That's it,* I thought. *That's the word to express what I've been facing for the last eight months.* Something had been rumbling inside of me, but now, finally, I had a word to describe what I had been experiencing.

Sometimes when we lose our footing, pausing, waiting, and seeming to do nothing can be the most helpful thing we can do if God leads us to that place of peace.

Finally, one day, only at the edges of my awareness at first, the darkness finally broke, and Jesus, the bright Morning Star, appeared once again. In that radiant light, I realized I was no longer the same. Despite my lack of trying to fix my situation, and the effort it took to not totally give up, I under-stood I had grown deeper emotionally and spiritually. It was peace.

[1] Ortberg, John. *Soul Keeping,* 2014, p.183.

Day 13

A Piece of Peace

Ava Pennington

"Peace I leave with you; my peace I give you. I do not
give to you as the world gives. Do not let your hearts be
troubled and do not be afraid."

(John 14:27 NIV)

There are times when I wish I had more peace—especially as I cared
for my husband during his terminal illness this past year. Ever feel
that way ... like you know God gives you peace, but sometimes
you just don't have *enough* peace?

The problem with wishing for more is that it implies peace is a
commodity—something we receive in measured amounts. But
peace is not a product to be purchased, or an item packaged in a
bag or box. Neither is peace the absence of violence. It's not simply
a lack of noise. And it's not freedom from disagreement.

Peace is a Person.

More than 2,700 years ago, Isaiah wrote of the coming of One who
is the Prince of Peace (Isaiah 9:6). The Prince of Peace, Jesus Christ,

entered this world of sin and discord for one purpose: He came to reconcile us to God—to restore a relationship broken by sin. The Prince of Peace came so we might have peace with God, with ourselves, and with others.

It's not a matter of having *more* peace. Either we have it—*Him*—or we don't. There's no continuum moving from little to more to much. So, when we wish for more peace, we might ask ourselves a few questions:

Am I at peace with God? Romans 5:1 (NIV) tells us that "since we have been justified through faith, we have peace with God through our Lord Jesus Christ."

Have you ever known the peace of being reconciled to God? If not, this is the first step. Give yourself the best gift possible—the assurance that you belong to your heavenly Father through the gift of the Prince of Peace.

Am I at peace with myself? Philippians 4:6-7 (NIV) reminds us, "Do not be anxious about anything, but in every situation, by prayer and petition, with thanksgiving, present your requests to God. And the peace of God, which transcends all understanding, will guard your hearts and your minds in Christ Jesus."

If peace with ourselves depends on our circumstances, then even though we've been reconciled to God, we may not be fully benefiting from His peace. Anxiousness, fear, and discouragement are indications we are viewing God from the perspective of our circumstances instead of viewing our circumstances from God's perspective.

Am I at peace with others? Romans 12:18 (NIV) tells us, "If it is possible, as far as it depends on you, live at peace with everyone."

Even while we were enemies of God, He gave His Son for us. We probably won't ever be asked to sacrifice our children for our enemies (aren't you glad of that?). However, God asks us to extend mercy to others, to look beyond our own hurts and be His hands and feet to a world that needs to know Him. We can't force others to accept it, but we *can* extend the hand of peace and leave the choice to them.

Peace—it's a gift that can come only from the One who *is* peace. Anything else is a poor imitation. Don't settle for a piece of peace. Enjoy God's precious gift of the Person of Peace.

Day 14

For Want of a Better Word— And a Word on a Better Want

Rhonda Rhea

"I consider everything a loss compared to the surpassing greatness of knowing Christ Jesus my Lord."

(Philippians 3:8 NIV)

Some people seem to have a way with words. Words, sentences, paragraphs—they all just flow out of them, all polished and pretty. Me not despising those people is a testament to how truly spiritual I am. (If you're not rolling your eyes right here, then you're obviously even more spiritual than I am. Impressive.)

Most of the time my words have to be coaxed, wheedled and prodded. My muse cops an attitude and is all like, "Not today, suckah." Then when I finally do get some words down, I still have to edit them up one side and down the other.

Writers of my caliber? We're the ones who want the words—written or spoken—all perfectly packaged. And we're constantly stepping back to look at the package, thinking things like, "That package really could've used a bigger bow. Maybe a red one. Perhaps an entirely different paper. Also … a different package altogether." Incidentally, we're the same people who spend a good minute and a half practicing to get the wording just right in our heads before ordering into the drive-through speaker.

Word-discontent. I have it often. I just edited those last few sentences, like, six times. Then still left "word-discontent" in there, pretending it's grammatically sound. And pretending it's actually a word.

Discontentment is a tricky rascal. All kinds of discontentment originate in thinking we need something different than we have. Something better. Something in a different package. Something with a red bow. Something more. And at every level of discontentment is that next little niggling thought that we will never be truly happy until we have that something more.

That kind of dissatisfaction always breeds conflict—within ourselves and with other people as well. "What is the source of wars and fights among you? Don't they come from the cravings that are at war within you?" (James 4:1, HCSB).

Are you warring with dissatisfaction—maybe even warring with others because of it? Want to change that? There's only one way to stop wanting more. And that is to want a different kind of more. More Jesus.

Wanting more of Jesus than anything else in life—that changes everything. Focusing on Him shines a light on any selfish wants and they're seen for the empty, unfulfilling distractions they really are.

Wanting more Jesus is a life pursuit. Maybe not so much coaxing, wheedling and prodding, but it is learned, day by day, and it requires our attention. As we give that attention to times of seeking the Lord's face in prayer, making His Word part of our everyday life and our everyday thinking, letting those connections with Him make us quick to get rid of sin, we find the temporary things of this world less appealing. And we find His love, His truth, His "Him-ness," so much more desirous than anything else we've ever known. (Yes, I just wrote the word, "Him-ness" in there—with nary an eye-roll.)

At that place of praise-filled closeness to Him, we're drawn into worship. It's impossible to worship in His fullness and still want what we're not supposed to want. In worship, we're reminded we truly do have everything we need. In Ephesians 1:3 (ESV), Paul praises the Father who "has blessed us in Christ with every spiritual blessing."

Discontentment? Bye-bye. Because … not today, suckah!

Wait, did I word that wrong?

Day 15

Counterintuitive Peace

Deborah McCormick Maxey, Ph.D.

"He will cover you with his pinions, and under his
wings you will find refuge."

(Psalm 91:4 NRSV)

"Brain surgery." Never had words produced so much anxiety in me. I had prayed the world renown team would suggest a pill. My mind constantly replayed the image of what it would entail to create a "hole in the head," scalpels in my grey matter and affixing a titanium plate.

It was the first week in December, and instantly I knew that other than my husband, who was with me, God was calling me to keep this scary news from everyone else. I could not let the joy of the Christmas holiday be marred with the idea that on New Year's Eve, I would undergo this procedure.

As worship leader and a prayer warrior, I was mystified by His direction. But eventually, I understood why the Lord led me not to ask for prayer. He wanted me to look up, not around, for support.

A few days later I felt called to private message a Facebook acquaintance whose sister is a pastor. Though we had never met, they advised me to memorize Psalm 91 and to think of it as "911" to God, because of his promises of protection featured there.

I began intense study. Verse by verse, I journaled deeply into the meaning of the words. As a visual person, it was not enough to understand what the Scripture said, I wanted images to spring to mind as I recited the words in praise and petition.

When I got to verse 4, "he will cover you with his pinions, and under his wings you will find refuge" (NRSV), I googled "Birds protecting their young" and found images that brought me peace. Parent birds stretch out their wings and shield their young beneath them. Huddled safe, the babes sleep peacefully while the parent bird stands watch.

Having always loved Bible references to angels, verses 11-12 brought great images that filled me with joy and wonder. "For he will command his angels concerning you to guard you in all your ways. On their hands they will bear you up" (NRSV).

Verse 15 promises He will not fail. "When they call to me, I will answer them; I will be with them in trouble, I will rescue them and honor them" (NRSV).

En route to Duke University on the day of surgery, the song, "This is the day that the Lord has made, I will rejoice and be glad in it," spontaneously repeated in my head. And unbelievably, I felt the truth of those words.

Before leaving for the hospital, I had written "Psalm 91" with a Sharpie in the palm of my hand, so I could grasp it like a squeeze ball if I needed extra strength. But there was an unintended effect: a member of the hospital staff saw it, recognized it, and many prayed with me on the spot. Afterward, folks I never met on the surgical team found me to say that they also saw it and prayed.

I suffer from a chronic neurological disorder, Trigeminal Neuralgia, also known as the "Suicide Disease" because seventy-two percent of those diagnosed end their lives within two years of onset. I trusted God to make a way. His answer was to reduce the 24/7 pain with very scary surgery. However, He knew all along that His grace would be sufficient when I sought Him through it.

Over time and prayer, we learn to discern His voice. Even when it seems counterintuitive, we must throw our trust on Him. He has a plan, a lesson, and a blessing in store through obedience. And His presence in our discipline brings peace.

Day 16

Last Straw at Walmart

Kathy Howard

"Come to me, all you who are weary and burdened, and
I will give you rest. Take my yoke upon you and learn
from me, for I am gentle and humble in heart, and you
will find rest for your souls. For my yoke is easy and my
burden is light."

(Matthew 11:28-30 NIV)

It had been a bad day. Issues with my family, issues at work, even
issues with my hair. I had complained to God and one of my close
friends. But I was pretty determined to be in a bad mood. I only
had one more errand before I could go home and wallow in self-
pity for the rest of the evening. Since I only needed a handful of
things from Walmart—milk, toilet paper, and fabric dye—I expected to be in and out in just a few minutes.

Storming around the store with my "poor me" attitude, I found
the fabric dye on the aisle with the laundry detergent. Dark brown
was only available in the liquid version. I needed a lot, so I started
pulling bottles off the little shelf over my head. Each time I grabbed

one, the others were pushed forward by a spring-loaded mechanism on the shelf.

As I lifted the next-to-last bottle, the one behind it shot out and up. There was no time to take cover, it all happened too fast. When the bottle hit the tile floor, the cap popped off and dark liquid squirted across the aisle splattering everything in its path, including me. As I surveyed the damage, God spoke to me quietly. "Okay, you've been whining all day. How are you going to respond to this?"

While I sponged myself off with the paper towels hung on a nearby post, I considered my options. I could continue down the path I'd been on all day and let this dark mess be the last straw that pushed me over the edge to a full-blown, self-absorbed tantrum. Or, I could remember that God is in control. He not only is aware of all the problems, issues, and worries in my life, He cares about each one.

In that moment of decision, God brought Matthew 11:28-30 to mind. He graciously offered to take my burden. To trade His "easy yoke" for the heavy weight I'd been dragging around all day. And the burden I might consider picking up the next day.

Rest in Jesus or throw a fit on the detergent aisle in Walmart? This time I chose Jesus. And I pray I will next time too. God's peace and rest is always available to His children amid chaos, trouble, and even the generic "bad" day. I still sometimes react to difficulty in my strength, but thankfully, I rest in God's peace more now than I did even a year ago.

On my way home, I called the sweet friend I had complained to earlier in the day. We both laughed as I recounted the flying dye story. Sometimes God uses unique ways to get our attention. On this day, He used a bottle of brown, liquid dye to remind me He was right there, waiting to carry my burden and give my weary soul some much needed rest.

Day 17

The Truth about Peace

Edie Melson

"I have said these things to you, that in me you may
have peace. In the world you will have tribulation. But
take heart; I have overcome the world."

(John 16:33 ESV)

I didn't have to experience the stress of our Marine Corps son's
deployment to know it was going to be a struggle. But it took that
experience for me to understand that finding peace didn't always
look and feel like I expected.

I thought peace was the absence of strife. To have peace meant
I had to control how I lived my life. If I kept a tight rein on my
environment, my diet and my exercise, I believed I'd be insulated
from the extremes of life.

But that deployment taught me *I* was not in control of my circumstances.

It forced me to re-evaluate my entire concept of living a tranquil
life. I didn't find that much-prized peace until I finally realized I
was looking in all the wrong places.

Peace, I discovered, wasn't an exterior thing, *it was an interior thing.*

Times of chaos will explode into our lives with ferocity. When this happens, our schedules, environment, or best-made plans crumble. We are compelled to acknowledge someone bigger than us at the helm.

We see many examples in the Bible of people at peace in the face of trouble. For instance, King David wrote Psalm 4 at a time of turmoil and frustration in his kingdom. Prominent citizens were openly ridiculing David and questioning God's wisdom in appointing him king.

How did David answer their fear and cynicism? He pointed them away from himself to the God who provided and controlled everything around them. It was confidence in Him that allowed David to remain at peace. "You have put gladness in my heart, more than when their grain and new wine abound. In peace I will both lie down and sleep, for You alone, O Lord, make me to dwell in safety" (Psalm 4:7-8 NASB).

In the New Testament, we see how Jesus experienced demanding crowds who pushed in, insisting on His attention. We watch as He dealt with disappointment when His followers fell short. We see when He faced the unexpected death of Lazarus and the terrible grief of His dear friends.

But through it all, Jesus exemplified a peace-filled life. And it had nothing to do with what was going on around Him, much less diet, exercise, or environment. It had everything to do with allowing God to direct His steps.

So whether you're facing a loved one's deployment or something else, I encourage you with the certainty that peace is possible. When we look first to God, we can always find tranquility, and the peace that comes with it.

Day 18

The Color of Sunshine

Carol Kent

"Friends, when life gets really difficult, don't jump to
the conclusion that God isn't on the job. Instead, be
glad that you are in the very thick of what Christ experienced. This is a spiritual refining process, with glory just
around the corner"

(1 Peter 4:12-13 THE MESSAGE).

It was the worst experience of my life. My boat had been rocked.
My confidence had eroded. I questioned my worth as a mother and
as a wife. If I could have curled up in the embryo position, fallen
asleep, and said goodbye to life, that would have been my choice.
No, I wasn't actually suicidal. I just didn't think there was much
about life that made it worth living.

My husband and I had received the devastating news that our son,
a graduate of the U.S. Naval Academy, had been arrested for a hei-
nous crime. The details surrounding this shocking announcement
took my breath away.

Most of us have had a phone call, a diagnosis from a doctor, a
financial reversal, a betrayal by a loved one, or a crisis in life that
made us question God's love for us, our value to others, and our
ability to go on with a normal life. That was me. I felt like standing

up and saying, "I quit life! It's too hard! I don't have the energy to fight anymore! I give up!"

In the middle of my despair, the doorbell rang. It was a delivery-man holding a covered object in his hand. With a cheery smile, he said, "Are you Carol Kent?"

I nodded.

"Well, it's your lucky day! Somebody must want to make you feel special today, and I'm delivering this gift. Enjoy your day!"

He disappeared as quickly as he came, and I held an object wrapped in green florist paper. As I tore away the protective covering, my eyes fell on one dozen of the most perfect yellow roses I had ever seen.

I opened the envelope. It was from two of my sisters. It read:

Dear Carol,

You once gave us some decorating advice. You said, "Yellow flowers will brighten any room." We thought you needed a little yellow in your life right now."

Love,

Bonnie and Joy

Suddenly, the skylight over my kitchen island revealed glorious sunshine pouring its rays on my beautiful bouquet. The yellow roses glistened in between the baby's breath and soft green fern, bringing an artistic glow to the unexpected gift.

Tears flooded my eyes, and I heard myself wailing like a mother mourning a great loss. I hadn't realized that I hadn't given my-self permission to grieve over my deep disappointment. I had been slapping on a fake smile, being strong for others, and masking my heavy heart. It was a moment of honest grief and for the first time in a long time, I willingly received support from others.

From that day on, yellow was my color for hope and peace.

If you're struggling with sorrow, hopelessness, or discouragement, review Psalm 77:1 (NIV): "I cried out to God for help; I cried out to God to hear me." It's important to be honest with Him. In our search for peace, we'll find renewed hope in His Word. And sometimes He sends encouragement through people who bring sunshine to our lives.

It's His way of saying: I see you. I hear your cry for help. I love you.

Day 19

I Want What She Has

Lori Wildenberg

"I have told you these things, so that in me you may have peace. In this world you will have trouble. But take heart! I have overcome the world."

(John 16:33 NIV)

My first-year teaching, I noticed my colleague in the classroom across the hall was not like anyone I had ever met. Her confidence, gentleness, and strength saturated calm into her classroom atmosphere and washed over those around her. She exuded peace. I wanted what she had. Her peaceful countenance was like honey. Its sweet, sticky goodness latched on to those (including me) around her.

Pat was my unofficial professional and spiritual mentor. As time unfolded, I realized the source of her peace—it was her never wavering faith in Jesus. She knew Jesus; she knew God's Word; she knew how to love God and others well. Her internal peace was externally evident in her interactions with her students. Her whole demure demonstrated *shalom*.

My first non-tenured year concluded; my job was finished at that school. I continued to teach in the same school district, only at different locations. A few years went by, and as God would have it, in an entirely different school He placed me across the hall from Pat again. This event was not lost on me. I knew God wanted to me to grow.

Even though my mid-twenty-self perceived her as nearly perfect, she openly revealed her imperfections with me. I was newly married, and she was transparent about her early years' marital struggles. I was suffering with infertility, and she came to my home on the weekend and prayed with me. She shared her feelings and fears with me about her miscarriage. She took time for me, loved me, shared her heart, and prayed with me. While I looked to her for direction, there were times she sought encouragement from me. Her investment in our relationship, her genuineness, her humility and love made a great impact on the development of my faith.

Looking back, I can see how effectively God used her to draw me to Him. The taste of security, safety, and contentment—some ingredients of peace—I got from her fed my hungry soul.

In a world filled with unrest, it is good to be reminded of the impact a peaceful spirit can have on another. Peacefulness is contagious. Most of us want to catch it. We desire tranquility, harmony, and security.

This side of heaven, those things won't be perfect, but they can cause us to seek the One who embodies shalom, Jesus Christ. Peace is a gift from God.

The manifestation of peace in a believer's life indicates a person's trust in God. My friend and colleague, Pat, was blessed with the gift of peace given due to her relationship with Him. She generously shared her gift of peace with her students and me.

I struggle a little, sometimes a lot, with allowing peace to permeate my heart. Perhaps it comes down to trusting God in hard situations. At those times, God reminds me of Pat.

Once peace rules in our heart and minds, others will be drawn to us. We will have the honor and privilege to share our shalom with them. They will want what we have.

Day 20

Peace in the Storm

Cheryl Hollar

"When I am afraid, I put my trust in you."

(Psalm 56:3 NIV)

"Behind the infection is some kind of cancer. The next 24 hours are critical ..."

As I heard the doctor's words, my jaw tightened.

It was 2014, on the day my twin sister and I were supposed to be enjoying ourselves at the annual International Twins Association's convention.

Endometrial cancer, stage 3c. That was the diagnosis. What followed was a nightmare of five surgeries and five and a half weeks in the hospital—three and a half of them in ICU. Complication after complication, including kidney failure, a surgical wound infection, atrial fibrillation, and difficulty in removing the breathing tube filled those weeks. With each complication or surgery, I thought I was saying goodbye to my twin, my built-in best friend. It was the darkest time of my life.

I was afraid. But I was not alone. My heavenly Father was by my side. I determined to follow David's example when he was captured by the Philistines: "When I am afraid, I put my trust in you" (Psalm 56:3 NIV).

God loves us, and He can be trusted.

He loves us more than we love ourselves, and He knows us inside and out. He knows our fears. And He *wants* us to depend on Him alone.

Letting go completely and trusting are very difficult things to do.

But God has proven over and over throughout time that He can be trusted with our biggest fears.

> When God called Moses to lead the children of Israel out of Egypt into the promised land, Moses was afraid. "What if they do not believe me or listen to me and say 'The LORD did not appear to you?'" (Exodus 4:1 NIV). But God proved faithful—from the sending of ten plagues on the Egyptians in Exodus 7:10-12:30 to their destruction at the parting of the Red Sea in Exodus 14:10-31. "The Lord will fight for you; you need only to be still"
>
> (Exodus 14:14 NIV).

Another time, Jesus was crossing the sea with the disciples in a boat when a fierce storm arose. The disciples were afraid for their lives and woke Jesus, who was asleep in the stern. The Bible tells us that "He got up, rebuked the wind and said to the waves, 'Quiet! Be still!' Then the wind died down and it was completely calm" (Mark 4:39, NIV).

We may not face a literal storm at sea or fight great earthly battles, but we daily—sometimes hourly—struggle with storms of doubt, worry, and uncertainty in our lives. We fear divorce and fear losing our jobs.

And we fear cancer.

God knows all about our struggles. He knows all about our fears.

He will see us through, either by healing or by simply being by our side through it all. He has promised never to leave us, never to forsake us. We can trust Him.

And my sister's cancer? I am truly humbled and grateful that God healed her and gave her back to me. He was by both our sides through radiation and chemotherapy. And on the eve of the fifth anniversary of her diagnosis, the cancer has not returned.

We thank God every day that we have each other. None of us knows when our time on earth will end, but when we are afraid, we can trust Him, no matter what the outcome or the cost.

One day, all will see *How Great Is Our God*.

Day 21

Will You Carry My Baggage, Please?

Donna Jones

"He committed no sin and no deceit was found in his mouth. When they hurled their insults at him, he did not retaliate; when he suffered, he made no threats. Instead, he entrusted himself to him who judges justly. He himself bore our sins in his body on the cross, so that we might die to sins and live for righteousness; by his wounds you have been healed."

(1 Peter 2:22-24 NIV)

While I was pregnant with our first child, my husband J.P. and I made a six-week trip to the middle of nowhere. Our first stop was a remote Malaysian island called Borneo, which is so off-grid it took four days to get there (and no, we didn't swim, but it might have been faster). Because our trip was lengthy, and because I was pregnant, and because we were young and stupid, we took entirely too much luggage.

The baggage issue wasn't really a problem for me, though. I had a hall pass from carrying heavy loads: pregnancy.

My delicate condition meant J.P. had to navigate Los Angeles, Tokyo, Singapore, Kuala Lumpur, Sibu, Hong Kong and Oahu with luggage in both hands, satchels slung over his shoulders, and a backpack large enough to carry a small village. We were a sight. Or rather, *he* was a sight. I skated from airport to airport, scot-free.

As we traveled from city to city, I'd occasionally glance at my weighted down husband, then glance down at my baggage-free body. I marveled at how he could carry so much junk—most of it mine—without a single word of complaint. Not once did he insist I carry my baggage. He *willingly* carried the burdens that were rightly mine.

Each time I looked at JP, and the ridiculous load of baggage slung all over his body, I knew one thing for sure: I was deeply, and fully, loved. Only love could motivate a person to bear a load not their own.

This is the love Jesus showed you and me. "He himself bore our sins in his body on the cross, so that we might die to sins and live for righteousness; by his wounds you have been healed" (1 Peter 2:24 NIV). Jesus willingly carried our baggage—our sin—on His own body, when He died on the cross. He carried the full weight of our sin, without a single word of complaint, and without a single sin of His own.

We all have baggage. Sadly, many of us travel through life picking up more baggage along the way; things like wounds, words, and worries. Hurt done to us. Guilt from the hurt we've done to others.

If we attempt to bear our own baggage, eventually we will crumble under the weight of our sin. In and of ourselves, we never find healing. We never find peace. We never find freedom.

The good news of Jesus is this: we don't need to carry the burden of our sin. Jesus carried it *all* to the cross.

When we look at the cross, with the ridiculous amount of baggage Jesus bore on His body there, may it remind us how deeply, and fully, we are loved.

Day 22

Peace When You Aren't Safe

A.C. Williams

"The Lord is good, a strong refuge when trouble comes.
He is close to those who trust in Him."

(Nahum 1:7 NLT)

The fajitas at the little Mexican restaurant in Hillsboro, Kansas, are tasty, but they aren't tasty enough to brave a tornado, which is exactly what happened the last time I ate there.

My best friend and I had just finished our meal when a massive rainstorm hit the restaurant. Since we'd been chatting, we had the volume on our phones turned down. But it was Kansas, and it was storm season, so I checked my phone quickly to see what the weather was doing. I found that I'd missed ten calls and fifteen text messages from many of my storm-chaser friends.

One friend was frantic, trying to find out where I was. I responded with my location as we went to pay for our meal. Just then, the power in the restaurant blinked off, and my phone alerted me to a new text message from my friend: "Not a safe place!"

My friend and I made a run for the car, since the restaurant was mostly glass and didn't have a storm shelter. Her family's farmhouse was a few minutes outside of town, and they had a crawlspace. Not ideal, but we figured that was our best option. We bolted to the car in the pouring rain and hail. As we got underway, the electrical systems in the car began flashing on and off. The further down the road we drove, the worse the wind became. And with every strike of lightning overhead, I could see the tendrils of ominous cloud dropping like black fingers from the sky on every side of us.

I'd never been through a tornado. I'd been close to them, seen them form from a distance, and witnessed the devastation they leave behind, but I'd never experienced one first-hand. Driving through this storm with the wind trying to blow us off the road, the rain pelting us so hard we couldn't see, and the funnel clouds descending on every side of us, I had never been more frightened.

But I'd never felt more at peace.

I knew, with no doubt, that if a tornado dropped on our heads, if we died right there, both my best friend and I would be just fine.

Nobody gets through life without facing storms (even the literal ones!), but with a relationship with God through Jesus Christ, we can face every obstacle with confidence. During our greatest challenges, we can hold on to the fact that there is always hope, because God is always with us. In the darkness of our most frightening storm, we can hold on to peace because God has promised to be our refuge when trouble comes (Nahum 1:7), and He always keeps His promises.

So the next time you find yourself in a place that isn't safe, remember that you aren't alone, and even when the storm gets scary, you can still have peace—God's peace.

As for me and my friend? Well, the tornado actually missed us. We got to her parents' house and were prepped to dive into the crawlspace if the pressure in the room changed, but it didn't. So we finished our fajitas out of our to-go box and watched the storm clouds roll past instead.

I'll never forget the lesson the Lord taught me in those terrifying moments as the funnel clouds dropped around us: sometimes you have to experience life's greatest fear and uncertainty before you can actually know the peace that comes from God.

Day 23

Chaotic Peace

Karen Wingate

"May the God of hope fill you with all joy and peace as
you trust in him, so that you may overflow with hope
by the power of the Holy Spirit."

(Romans 15:13 NIV)

During a season of productive outreach events, the church my
husband pastors suffered an eight month-long, unrelenting roll-
er coaster: life-threatening health diagnoses, families in crisis, and
staff problems.

Then the worst happened. The elder serving as chairman of our
flourishing missions committee, who was a close friend to me and
my husband, disappeared. Two weeks later, his body surfaced in
a nearby lake, leaving behind a seriously ill wife and a distraught
congregation.

News spread fast, and churches across the country prayed for our
little isolated congregation. After telling me that her midweek Bible study had prayed for us, my sister added, "I hope God is flooding you with His peace."

The dam broke. I texted back: "I don't feel peace. I don't feel comfort. I don't feel strong. Right now, I'm going on sheer faith."

What would peace in these circumstances feel like, anyway? I wondered. This situation wasn't going anywhere fast, anytime soon. We hurt and we would hurt for a long time.

I held weeping women in my arms as they asked, "Why?"

We learned to cling to the only two things we had—faith that God understood the whys and wherefores even if we did not and sharing the burden of grief as we took turns faltering and regaining our grip.

Romans 15:13 promises that joy and peace will come because of our trust in God, which will in turn lead to an abundance of hope. Peace, I came to realize, is not a feeling. It is not a state of circumstances, either. It is contentment with that gut-deep assurance that God is who He says He is, and He will keep His promises even if everything around me screams otherwise.

Proverbs 18:10 describes it best when Solomon wrote, "The name of the Lord is a strong fortress; the godly run to him and are safe (NLT)." He got that idea from his father, David, who wrote in Psalm 46:1, "God is our refuge and strength, always ready to help in times of trouble (NLT)."

The elder's death didn't make sense to us. We had no answers. But we knew the One who did. Like a child who hunkers down into its mother's arms during a severe thunderstorm, we could find security in Him and believe in His words, "I have overcome the world (John 16:33, NIV)."

Peace does not come when everything settles down and troubles subside. The war still rages, and the wind still rips through the rafters. We find safety and rest when we put our trust and confidence in the One who knows the big picture of the battle and reigns supreme over the storm.

Neither does peace come in perfect circumstances, perfect relationships, or in our own perfect righteousness. It is a by-product of trust and belief in a perfect God who knows all, sees all, and loves us in infinite detail despite it all.

As our congregation learned to seek shelter through our faith in a God who would not let us fall or fail, hope returned. The unresolved chaos of our broken world still existed, but we found sanctuary in the sovereignty of God.

When life beats you down, when the worst follows what is already bad, stick close to Jesus. Recommit yourself to Him every day as you put one foot in front of the other. God knows what is happening to you. He cares. He has the strength to pull you through the dark moments. In that, you will find contentment and peace.

Day 24

God's Divine Tactics

Carole Lewis

"The weapons we fight with are not the weapons of the world. On the contrary, they have divine power to demolish strongholds"

(2 Corinthians 10:4 NIV).

The Bible says Satan wants to kill, rob, and destroy—these are his tactics. God's Word, on the contrary, tells us, "The weapons we fight with are not the weapons of the world. On the contrary, they have divine power to demolish strongholds" (2 Corinthians 10:4 NIV).

So it is very important we learn how to focus on God's tactics—which are to give us good gifts that give us life and build us up.

Our middle child, Shari, was tragically killed on Thanksgiving night, 2001, by an 18-year-old girl who was driving drunk. Her car left the street and struck our daughter who was standing behind their family car preparing to go home after having dinner at her in-laws' home. Shari and Jeff and their three girls, nineteen, fifteen, and thirteen, had spent the day with us at our home at the bay, and Shari had decorated my Christmas tree as she always did before they left for dinner at Jeff's parents.

After Shari's death, I have been able to see God's tactics at work in our family. God helped me write 90 devotionals in eight days, just six weeks after Shari died. I was still in shock, but today when I read one of those devotionals, I know this is some of my best writing, because God did it. The writing was also wonderful therapy too. I wrote *A Thankful Heart* from a list I had made after Shari's death of every time I saw God's hand working in our lives.

The morning after Shari's death, Shari's oldest daughter, Cara, received her acceptance letter to Texas A & M University. Admission to this college was a great gift to us all, because we knew this was the desire of her heart to study there. And there was more.

Cara put her name into the lottery for a roommate because she felt that people she didn't know would be more accepting if she was sometimes distant or withdrawn because of her mother's death.

The day Cara moved into her dorm, our staff was praying for her because it was just six weeks since her mom died. I had shared that Cara wouldn't be able to get the counseling she needed and one of our staff suggested, "Why don't we pray?" Well, wouldn't you just know what God would do in this situation? He gave Cara a Christian roommate and two Christian suitemates. One of the suitemates had also tragically lost her mother just a few days after she turned 18, during her senior year of high school. God used His divine tactics in Cara's life to show her how much He loved her, even in the midst of loss.

As Christians we belong to God. Yes, the weapons of this world are terrible. It is comforting, though, to know that we are not the ones doing the fighting. What is true for Cara—and for me—is also true for you. We can rest in peace because God has every situation all worked out for us. He worked it out before the foundation of the world.

Day 25

No Longer Fatherless

Lee Ann Mancini

"A father of the fatherless and a judge for the widows, is God in His holy habitation."

(Psalm 68:5 NASB)

When I was eighteen, my father died of lung cancer. He had been absent during my childhood, and I had always longed to hear what his voice sounded like or to see his face. But before I could meet him, he died. This affected every aspect of my life and caused great heartache.

I had a wonderful mother who did her best to be both mother and father to me, but I never stopped longing for him. When I saw my childhood friends with their dads, I would ask, "Can you be my dad, too?" As an adult, I continued longing for a dad who would affirm his love and help me feel confident and secure. One who would stand beside me when I faced life's dilemmas and trials.

Now I could never say "I love you, Dad." Father's Day brought a sad reminder each year of what was never to be.

So I thought.

When I accepted Jesus as my Savior, my longing was unexpectedly fulfilled; in that moment, I also gained my heavenly Father.

Psalm 68:5 NASB states God is a

"Father of the fatherless." The hole in my heart is
now filled with the love of my Father God.

He is perfect. He is my protector, my provider, my sustainer, and He wraps His loving arms around me when I need Him, even in the middle of the night, when my mind will not rest. He fulfills all that has been lost or stolen by the enemy.

Yes, it was sad not to have my dad walk me down the aisle on my wedding day, but my Heavenly Father will one day give me the hand of His Son Jesus. I have already inherited His name and His kingdom.

I have gradually realized I am truly without need of anything.

This understanding transforms me daily. I am becoming a woman who is less stressed, worried, and anxious, with freedom to share God's love and message of salvation with others. I am not merely a mother, wife, author, teacher, or speaker, because those titles only define my experience here on earth. I am the daughter of God, the creator of all things.

My true identity is what the Father has claimed me to be: the bride of His Son.

I no longer struggle with my looks, my identity, my purpose, or my self-worth. I know my present times of trouble are nothing compared to what awaits me in glory. As I look in the mirror, I can almost see the wedding crown on my head that was paid for by the crown of thorns, because my heavenly Dad loves me!

Whenever I revert to past lost feelings, God reassures me in His Word that He is indeed my Father,

"And I will be a father to you, and you shall be sons and daughters to me" (2 Corinthians 6:18 NASB). I do not have to be afraid; I am not a fatherless child anymore.

Jesus told His disciples, "Do not be afraid, little flock, for your Father has chosen gladly to give you the kingdom"

(Luke 12:32 NASB).

I praise the Lord for loving me and taking care of me. My heart no longer longs for an earthly dad; what I once lost is now replaced with the love and hope my Heavenly Father gives to me daily. He is my Abba, Father, my great reward, my everything!

Day 26

Making the Most of a Broken Relationship

Janet Chester Bly

"He heals the brokenhearted and binds
up their wounds."

(Psalm 147:3 NASB)

Two friends of mine found very different ways through their relationship ordeals.

Evene struggled to the point of deep depression when her husband left her. One day after returning home from church, she decided to get back on a spiritual track. "I opened my Bible for the first time in a long while. So many Scriptures came alive to me in new ways. I pored over the places I'd underlined and highlighted in happier days. I thumbed my Bible to ragged edges. Out of these precious moments, I eventually released my husband to the Lord and trusted He was in control of it all. I still have hard times, but God's grace shines in so many ways, giving me strength, peace, and love for others despite my agony."

Then there's Kathy. In the despair of several unhealthy relationships, Kathy felt she'd lost God. No one could console her. Her limited knowledge of a heavenly Father was from concepts she'd grasped as a child at Sunday School, the scope of her dysfunctional experiences, and a few Bible verses she recalled.

Now God seemed unreachable. Yet she craved a deep river of peace—a way out of her inner turmoil and outer chaos. She wanted God back. Her dark pit made her ripe for belief, to dare to hope God was out there, somewhere.

Then God sent a new friend, Mavis, who reached out to her and stuck with her through the rest of her trials.

Mavis suggested she read Psalm 77, which Kathy did, over and over. Amid her pain, anger, and confusion, she finally relaxed into God's peace, the peace that transcends all understanding (Philippians 4:7).

Praying for God's wisdom, she broke down the many issues she faced into bite-size pieces. God gave her insight and cleared her mind. She finally felt peace and received the miracle of compassion. God transformed Kathy's excessive pride into humility. With Mavis's encouragement and support, Kathy reached out to someone she knew she had hurt the most.

And God worked a wonder.

Our loving Father is aware of our every pain. Whether we've been dealt with unfairly or a broken relationship is our own fault, God aims in His good timing to bring us a good end to our story ... "deepening your understanding of every good thing we share for the sake of Christ" (Philemon 1:6 NIV).

God is not a bull in a china shop that crashes through, knocking us down in clumsy attempts to communicate. He brings peace. He speaks softly and extends goodwill with gentle touches. He knows how to deal with sensitivity in delicate issues.

> Psalm 145:9 (KJV) tells us, "The Lord is good to all:
> and his tender mercies are over all his works."

When we release our relationship dramas to Him, He surprises us with the unexpected. Perhaps there's total healing and blessed bliss. Or the change may only happen in our hearts. Either way, God gets the glory. We become honest, groping pilgrims, rather than the people with all the answers.

Dear Lord, You are not the source of our pain. You are our comfort. Help us know how to share with others what You've done for us. I believe in Your goodness, even in my despair. Putting one foot in front of the other, I'll keep moving forward until I've passed through this blackness.

Adapted from *Grace Spilling Over*, released 2020, © Janet Chester Bly

Day 27

Peace in the Wilderness

Julie Zine Coleman

"I will make a covenant of peace with them … so that
they may live in the wilderness and sleep in the forests
in safety. I will make them and the places surrounding
my hill a blessing. I will send down showers in
season; there will be showers of blessing."

(Ezekiel 34:25-6 NIV)

She was alone and afraid. Her homeland lay hundreds of miles
beyond the harsh Negev Desert. The cruel wilderness had already
taxed her strength and taken a toll on her pregnant body. Things
couldn't be grimmer.

Hagar had spent the last decade or so as a slave. She was pregnant
with the child of her master, who had used her as a surrogate to
bear the heir his wife could not. Hagar had made the mistake of
behaving badly toward the barren wife, flaunting her ability to con-
ceive. The wife's ensuing harsh treatment had made Hagar's life unbearable. She could stand it no longer. So she fled the compound,
determined to never return.

Now she was in the wilderness, without hope and few options.
It was the most desperate time in her life. But it was there God

would reveal Himself to her and establish a relationship that would change the course of her days.

Hagar's wilderness experience is echoed throughout Scripture. God called Abraham into the wilderness to establish a special relationship with Him and his descendants. Several hundred years later, God introduced Himself to Moses in the wilderness, this time in a burning bush. Not long after, the entire Hebrew nation left Egypt behind and traveled into the wilderness. There God established His covenant with them. Then He provided for their needs in the desert with manna and water.

There are others. The prophet Elijah went into the wilderness to die, overcome with discouragement and fear. God met him there, provided for his needs, and revealed Himself. John the Baptist did his preaching in the wilderness, not in a populated area as you might expect someone would when carrying such an important message. People came out in droves from the towns. There in the wilderness they met with God in a way they never had before, heeding the call to turn their hearts back to God and establishing a new relationship with Him.

The wilderness is a harsh, dry place, desolate in its emptiness and devoid of sustenance. Those in Scripture who found themselves there eventually understood their complete dependence on God, which softened their hearts to be ready to receive. God then revealed Himself in a new way, enabling a new or deeper relationship with Him. He met their immediate needs, then revealed His purpose and the ways He intended to bless them.

Have you ever found yourself in the wilderness? A time when things have gone to worms, leaving you desperate and without hope? Or maybe your circumstances didn't change, but inwardly you struggled with spiritual dryness, a lacking in reassurance of God's presence?

God purposefully brings us to that place many times in the course of our lives. A stint in the wilderness leads us to cry out to Him in desperation. There He then meets our need, proving his faithfulness and kind intentions toward us. In short, God uses the wilderness to deepen our understanding of Him and fill us with a new sense of purpose.

The wilderness is not a punishment. It is an opportunity. God calls us from the comfort of our normal circumstances to a deeper, more meaningful relationship with Him. He has great plans for you. Plans for your ultimate good. Plans for you to participate in His purposes. And He will use our experiences in the wilderness to accomplish them.

Day 28

When the *If Onlys* Make You Cross-eyed

Kathy Collard Miller

"Forgetting what is behind and straining toward what is ahead, I press on toward the goal to win the prize for which God has called me heavenward in Christ Jesus."

(Philippians 3:13b-14 NIV)

Someone has said, "If you have one eye on yesterday and the other eye on tomorrow, you'll look at today cross-eyed."

That's what regrets do to us. They give us a cross-eyed lack of peace.

It happens when we stop looking to the cross and the grace that saved us. We attempt to take back our guilt and shame by rehearsing our regrets from the past. Being stuck in the past keeps us from thinking positively about God's present working. We soon become discouraged about the future.

In fact, regrets are a form of worry—we worry with thoughts like, "If only I had treated my child better" or "If only I hadn't said that to my friend." Such "worry" keeps us from trusting God and keeps us trapped in our past regrets.

97

What can we do to fight against our many "if onlys …"?

That was my question over forty years ago, after God delivered me from being a child abuser. The thought of any possible emotional damage I had inflicted on my toddler daughter plagued me. *Can she ever be a loving human being? Can she ever love me? Will she blame God for what I did? Will she struggle with anger?*

Even though I had become a patient mom, and my marriage had been restored to a loving relationship, those thoughts continued to haunt me. The *if onlys* stole my peace. Until God helped me put His biblical solutions into practice.

One of them was noticing the Apostle Paul's perspective. He could have easily struggled with regrets—yet, he wrote, "Forgetting what is behind and straining toward what is ahead, I press on" (Philippians 3:13b-14 NIV).

Rather than meaning to "not remember," *forget* means "not be held hostage by." Paul is saying his readers shouldn't be held captive by the past. We can learn things from our past mistakes. But we should never allow those bad memories to keep us from moving forward.

Another key to overcoming regrets is in learning to forgive. We must extend mercy not only to others but also to ourselves. After all, God has extended mercy to us already for what we have done. It is a choice to stop focusing on the hurt we inflicted and the hurt others have inflicted upon us. Our enemy, Satan, wants us to become mired in regret, tearing ourselves down with discouraging lies. That guilt is not from God, who has removed our guilt from us permanently. When we go back to our past bad choices, we are not entertaining God's truths; we are only digging ourselves into a pit of depression.

Isaiah 43:25 can motivate us to receive His forgiveness. God says, "I, even I, am he who blots out your transgressions, for my own sake, and remembers your sins no more" (NIV). I was struck by the phrase, "for my own sake." I realized, *Lord, You have already forgiven me so that You could have fellowship with me—because You love me so much. It's not just for my benefit, but Yours as well. I receive Your forgiveness.*

God wants us to embrace His forgiveness and empower you for godly living. When you do, you will no longer be looking at life cross-eyed! You'll be filled with peace beyond your expectations.

By the way, none of my fears about my daughter occurred. She's a loving wife, wonderful mother, and serves God with love and joy. We are best friends. God was faithful to heal those wounds.

Day 29

The More You Pick Up, the More You Lay Down

Michelle Lazurek

"As Pharaoh approached, the Israelites looked up, and there were the Egyptians, marching after them. They were terrified and cried out to the LORD … 'It would have been better for us to serve the Egyptians than to die in the desert!' Moses answered the people, 'Do not be afraid. Stand firm and you will see the deliverance the LORD will bring you today. The Egyptians you see today you will never see again. The LORD will fight for you; you need only to be still.'"

(Exodus 14:10-14 NIV)

When my husband was a little boy, he enjoyed playing cards with his grandfather. His favorite game was Rummy 500. Players take turns picking up a card, then discarding one into the discard pile. When a player accumulates three matching (or sequential) cards, he can lay those cards down. Eventually a winner ends the game by emptying his hand completely.

Often, his grandfather would pick up many cards in the discard pile, only to get one set of three. When my husband asked him why he did that, he said, "The more you lay down, the more you can pick up."

This seemed counterintuitive to my husband. Wouldn't it make more sense to pick up less so he could better control the outcome? How could fill your hand result in winning a card game that rewarded an empty hand?

But it wasn't the cards his grandfather *picked up* that led to his wins. It was what he *laid down*. My husband could have picked up many cards in the pile, too. But having them in his hand when his grandfather discarded his last card would cause him to lose.

It's only when he laid them down that he ensured success.

In the above verse, the Israelites were afraid and cried out to the Lord for His help. The great Egyptian army coming at them seemed insurmountable. They simply could not fight this battle and win.

But Moses informed them the solution to the problem was not in picking up their weapons. Rather, they needed to put their trust in God. It was in their choice to be still that He would do what only He could do. He would win the battle for them. They just needed to stand by and watch.

So often, when we face a battle, we try everything in our power to control and manipulate a positive outcome for our circumstances. It's not until we surrender our lives to God that we can truly achieve the peace God desires for us.

It's what we lay down that allows peace. In our stillness before Him, we will see Him at work, doing what we never could have done.

Day 30

Jehovah Shalom, Lord of Our Peace

Sheryl Giesbrecht Turner

"For God is not a God of disorder but of peace."

(1 Corinthians 14:33 NIV)

Awake at 3:00 am, thoughts rolled around in my mind about the hard conversations I should have had but avoided. I was struggling over a staff decision that had been made for me. I wasn't invited into the discussion, nor did I have a say in the matter. My opinion was not considered.

I felt alone, misunderstood and misrepresented. The inky blackness of the night usually soothed me to sleep, but this night, the dark compounded my fears. Closing my eyes, all I could see was the threatening faces of the two people who ended my position at a job I loved.

"Lord, I don't understand this at all, but I trust You, I submit to you, and ask You for peace." Soon, I fell into a deep sleep. Waking up a few hours later, I felt the presence of Jehovah-Shalom. The God of peace had given me peace by consoling my soul. Instead of thinking in broken sentences, I now sang for joy. As I chose to praise God before the answer, I knew the battle was won. I felt confident, purposeful, and convinced He had chosen me for a greater work.

Jehovah-Shalom is the name of God that means I am the Lord your Peace. God spoke to Gideon while he was thrashing wheat, hiding from the enemy. He called Gideon a mighty warrior and assured him He would give him the victory when he led the troops into battle.

Through the peace he received, Gideon found strength to do what God had called him to do. "Gideon built an altar to the Lord there and called it "The Lord is Peace" (Judges 6:24 NIV). The Hebrew phrase translated "The Lord is Peace" is *Jehovah-Shalom* and occurs only once in the Old Testament.

Shalom is *harmony of relationship or a reconciliation.* Jesus is the Prince of Peace, because through His death and resurrection, He brought peace with God to anyone who believed in Him. The Lord continues to be a God of peace even in the midst of overwhelming odds.

When you feel as if God has abandoned you, choose to rest in the truth of what He says: He will be our peace. "Peace I leave with you; my peace I give to you; not as the world gives do I give to you. Do not let your heart be troubled, nor let it be fearful" John 14:27 NASB. His peace is available for the asking.

Jehovah Shalom gives peace in every situation, but especially when we feel lost, overlooked, weak, and inadequate. He keeps us in perfect peace when our minds are fixed on Him (see Isaiah 26:3). Choose peace, not chaos. Invite the peace of God to rule in your heart, mind and soul.

Heavenly Father, thank You that Jesus is my peace. When I have anxiety and fear I can pray Philippians 4:6-7 NLT, "Don't worry about anything, instead, pray about everything. Tell God what you need and thank Him for all He has done. If you do this, you will experience God's peace." Thank You for reconciling me to You, Lord, giving me peace of mind, through divine favor. Thank You, that like Gideon, You say to me, "The Lord is with you, Mighty Warrior." In Jesus name, amen.

Day 31

Safe Where I Belong

Peggy Sue Wells

"For the Son of Man has come to seek and to save that
which was lost."

(Luke 19:10 NASB)

One spring day, I played with my two-year-old grandson in the
backyard. When a noise caught his attention, the little boy turned
toward the street.

"Get back here," I called. "You are naughty and going into time out
for the rest of your life. Now, think about what you've done, and
how you will fix it!"

Are you scandalized by my response? Understandable. But how often do we think God responds to our choices and messes in this
angry fashion?

Of course, I did not really speak those soul-wounding words. Instead, I came alongside him as he toddled in an unsafe direction.

"Hey, buddy," I said gently. "Let's go back where you are safe." He
turned into my arms, I scooped him up, and in that instant, he was
safe. Cuddling this sweet bundle of boy, I carried him to his favor-

ite toys in the protected yard where he belonged, and we continued to laugh and play.

When my child explores beyond safe boundaries, makes unwise choices, or disobeys, I don't demand she grovel, do penance, or humiliate herself to satisfy my displeasure. But I am overjoyed when she hears my voice and turns into my embrace. Then I carry her to safety.

I have learned appreciation for how easily God offers to reconcile our relationship compared to how I previously thought the process worked. I believed asking God to forgive me must include groveling and then muscling myself into alignment with God's perfect will. I thought I had to prove authentic sorrow and sincere desire for forgiveness. But now I know forgiveness is already mine. And I gladly run into His arms for help when I've gotten myself into trouble.

Luke describes the terrible day Jesus was hung on a cross. He had been put there alongside two criminals, also sentenced to death. "One criminal who hung there hurled insults at him, 'Aren't you the Messiah? Save yourself and us!'

"But the other criminal rebuked him, saying, "Don't you fear God,' he said, 'since you are under the same sentence? We are punished justly, for we are getting what our deeds deserve. But this man has done nothing wrong.' Then he said, 'Jesus, remember me when you come into your kingdom.'

"Jesus answered him, 'Truly, I tell you, today you will be with me in paradise'" (Luke 23:39-43 NIV).

To receive forgiveness and eternal life, the thief on the cross did not get baptized, take communion, do good deeds, grovel, or clean the mess he had made that resulted in his crucifixion. Like my grandson, he simply turned into the outstretched arms. In that instant, the thief was secure. For eternity.

Like me, have you ever wandered off, stomped off in anger, drifted away in heartbreak, and become lost from relationship with God?

When I've made a mess of my choices, my life, my relationships, and with God, there is no way I can fix or even polish my problems. I can't find my way back on track to God.

Restoration is a simple turn away. Knowing I am incapable of securing salvation, God is always near with arms open in invitation and welcome. Like my grandson, who simply turned into my hug, I repent by turning into God's embrace and in that instant, I am safe where I belong. My gracious Savior already did the work of reconciliation and cleanup on the cross. Immediately, I receive God's gift of grace, security, and unconditional love.

Day 32

Do You Want Peace?

Gari Meacham

"When Jesus saw him lying there and *knew* that he had already been a long time in that condition. He said to him 'Do you wish to get well?"

(John 5:6 NASB) emphasis mine.

Lying on a dirty mat next to the pool at Bethsaida, this man had little hope of obtaining the healing Jews believed was in the waters. He said, "'I have no one to help me into the pool when the water is stirred. While I am trying to get in, someone else goes down ahead of me'" (John 5:7 NASB).

If Jesus already knew (as it states in verse 6) he had been lying there for a long time, why did He ask the probing question, "Do you want to get well?"

Jesus asks us the same question. "Do you want to get well? Do you want freedom? Do you want peace?"

When we ask God to restore our marriage or heal our body, plead with Him to keep our kids out of trouble, or get on our knees asking for harmony and reconciliation in our family, His answer and

His love for us isn't dependent on how well we behave. He loves us no matter what, but He invites us to take action. "Pick up your mat and walk" (John 5:8 NASB).

This page in John chapter five in my Bible has been so loved, so cried on, so pored over it has ripped in two. Yellowing tape holds it together and the corner of the page has been turned so many times that it now has a jagged edge. This Scripture has deep personal meaning for me as the daughter of a paralyzed man. After my dad's car accident, he lived in a wheelchair, possessing little movement in his hands and arms and no movement in his legs. I watched him clamp down on his arm brace with his teeth so he could hold a fork or grasp a comb. He waited in his hospital bed for a nurse to get him up in the morning, and he waited at night to be put to bed.

Toward the end of my father's life, his heart was giving out, and most of his bodily functions were failing. He spent the last few weeks of his life away from the small mountain hospital where he'd lived and in a Denver hospital close to me, my sister, my brother, and my mom. We were so happy to have those weeks with him, whispering sweet stories to him and holding his hands as we visited.

When he passed away, I realized my dad had been in his paralyzed condition for exactly thirty-eight years. The precise number of years this man in the Bible had lived with mangled limbs.

Once in a while someone will ask me about my dad. What about his healing? Didn't he, too, want to get well? Dad and I once had this conversation. I was young and headstrong, feeling quite convinced that the sure sign of healing was only what could be seen physically. My dad felt otherwise. He explained he had peace with God, and so he lived his life with quiet reserve from the seat of his wheelchair.

Tethered to a chair, yet free with his God.

"For He Himself is our peace" (Ephesians 2:14 NASB).

Adapted from *Spirit Hunger* by Gari Meacham, Zondervan, 2012. Used by permission

Day 33

Who's Your Referee?

Sharon Tedford

"Let the peace of Christ rule in your hearts, to which
indeed you were called in one body; and be thankful."

(Colossians 3:15 NASB)

I love soccer. I grew up in a house where soccer *is* the Saturday
event. It's not a sport I've ever participated in, but I've watched
and cheered at many games. The speed of the play, the roar of the
crowd, and the meat pies at half time (can you spot my English
roots here?) make for an afternoon of rambunctious fun you don't
want to miss!

The referee of a soccer match needs to have his (or her) head
screwed on tight, as soccer players are not known for their gentle
words or actions. Regardless of the opinion of the players, if a referee gives an order or directive, they would be wise to listen. Those
who struggle with this voice of authority will face consequences.

It's the same with any referee, umpire, judge, or linesman. What
they say goes! The referee follows the rules to which all participants
have agreed and helps the players stick to the same standard. I guess
you could say he is the "plumb line." It would be ridiculous to

expect the goalie or the crowd to be the ones who keep everyone on the pitch (the field) in order during the game. The match can only run smoothly when everyone plays by the same rules.

As a Jesus follower, what rules do I live by? Do I let the way I feel in the moment rule? Or perhaps I let the standard set by the majority rule my responses? Maybe I even let the desire for being right rule me?

In Colossians 3:15 (NASB), we see an enlightening parallel for those of us who are on "Team Jesus." It's no accident the phrase, "Let the peace of God rule" is central to this well-known Scripture. When we choose to wrap everything we do around His peace, we are more effective *players*. When we all make His peace our plumb line, we can be a *team* who functions with unity and kindness.

The Father invited each of us to be on His team, and He wants us to sign up to function in godly peace. Just as soccer players all agree to follow the same rules, I want to be a Christian who participates as a team player. When I spend time with my teammates and learn how to respond and react to them in the best way possible, I will be part of a group who are (much like the soccer team) all running towards the same goal.

I choose to put God's peace at the very center of my heart. When we let God's peace rule, we are choosing unity with each other. And, as noted at the end of the Scripture above, a unified team of Christians is something to very special.

We must determine to allow the peace of God to rule our hearts, our actions, and even our thoughts. Only when we *let* peace rule, will we be able to love each other well (Colossians 3:14). So, let us be a team that submits to His standard, as we peacefully move together as one body; one united team that brings the vitally important message of Jesus to the world.

Day 34

Jesus Took My Burden

Fran Caffey Sandin

"Humble yourselves, therefore, under God's mighty
hand, that he may lift you up in due time. Cast all your
anxiety on him because he cares for you."

(1 Peter 5:7 NIV)

With a quivering voice, I said into the phone, "Dr. Burk, I don't
know what to do. Steve said he doesn't want to go back to the
hospital, but he is still struggling to breathe. What do you think?"

He responded, "I trust your judgment, and you can do whatever
you believe is best. I am giving you my cell number—call me anytime you need my advice."

Wow! The burden of anxiety weighed profoundly on my heart.
What decision should I make?

Steve, our young adult son with cystic fibrosis, had been hospital-
ized for three weeks for treatment of a severe pulmonary fungal
infection that would take a full six months of medication to completely eradicate. But the first evening at his townhouse, Steve was
still suffering. What should I do?

The word *burden* kept coming to mind. Steve had trouble taking a satisfactory breath of air, even while receiving supplemental oxygen, and I felt a heaviness in my chest. Although gripped with fear and uncertainty, I reassured Steve, "Dr. Burk said it is okay to try to make it through the night here, and I can call him as needed."

It was then that I recalled the chorus of an old hymn.

> *Jesus took my burden I could no longer bear*
>
> *Yes, Jesus took my burden in answer to my prayer.*
>
> *My anxious fears subsided, my spirit was made strong,*
>
> *For Jesus took my burden and left me with a song.* *

I began singing the words for myself and for my son, too. Then I remembered Steve had ordered a Jewish prayer shawl with the names of God embroidered along the edge. I said, "Steve, I am spreading this prayer shawl over your shoulders while I pray in faith, believing the Lord will see us through the night."

"Dear Father, I come to You in the name of my Lord and Savior, Jesus Christ, thanking You for inviting us to come boldly to Your throne of grace. I confess You are Jehovah Rapha, the God who heals, Jehovah Jireh, the God who provides. Now I pray in the power of our resurrected Lord that You will have mercy on Steve tonight and bring relief and healing to Steve's lungs so he can rest. In Jesus' precious name I pray, Amen.

By this time, while wiping away my tears, I felt the power of God's spirit in our midst. I gently removed the prayer shawl and noticed within minutes that Steve seemed more relaxed. Yes! Jesus had taken my burden and Steve's, too. His color gradually improved, and he began breathing better. I performed percussion treatments on his back periodically to help dislodge mucous, checked on him throughout the night, and rejoiced at sunrise. Dr. Burk had asked me to let him know what happened, and when I called with the report, he was pleased.

The King James version of 1 Peter 5: 7 reads, "Casting all your care upon Him for He cares for you." In casting we are to throw, fling, toss, launch, or let fly. Basically, let the anxiety go. Instead of worrying and fretting, we can pray and let Jesus walk with us through our difficult circumstances. God promises we are never alone, and He is always our source of peace. To God be the glory!

Jesus Took My Burden, hymn by Rev. John Oatman, Jr. and Bertha Mae Lillenas, copyright 1933. From the Cokesbury Worship Hymnal, 1959, page 45. Public Domain.

Day 35

At the End of Myself

Lynn Eib

"You will keep in perfect peace all who trust in you, all whose thoughts are fixed on you!"

(Isaiah 26:3 NLT)

Ever had a week when you felt really overwhelmed and alone? Here's mine:

My youngest daughter's two-year-old, four-year-old and husband had the flu, while her six-month-old had a double ear infection. My middle daughter was tending to her two flu-stricken preschoolers, following her own and her kindergartener's illness bouts. My oldest daughter's best friend was struck by a car while jogging and in trauma care fighting for her life.

My prayer partner of many years was recovering from the flu and couldn't get off the couch. My closest friend from church was unreachable as she vacationed abroad. Another close friend was stuck in Colorado with a totaled car.

My husband was still recovering with a knee replacement and couldn't walk or drive without great pain.

And did I mention that while working on my taxes, I discovered an error resulting in *several thousand dollars* of unpaid taxes, penalty fees galore, and a possible lien being put on our home?

Guess who wasn't feeling much peace? That's right, the one who's read every single peace verse in different Bible translations and wrote a *whole book* about seeking and finding peace.

As I stressed over tax deadlines, FB book launch posts, blogs, magazine articles, speaking engagement preparations, and concern for so many loved ones in difficult circumstances, any peace I had vanished.

I tried to practice what I "preached" in my book and made efforts to be "good" to myself. I got a massage. I went for walks. I relaxed in my hot tub. I ate a big bowl of popcorn. I drank a root beer float *with* the popcorn. But I still wasn't feeling it.

I prayed. I read my Bible. I listed to Jordan Smith sing "Great is Thy Faithfulness" on my iPhone. But even *The Voice* winner couldn't deliver my elusive peace.

So I texted my friend Gigi, who lives out West, and told her I was really stressed and asked her to call me that weekend. We've been friends for 40 years and she always can make me laugh. Within moments, my phone beeped (while I was talking to the tax debt collector!).

"You must be really desperate to want me to call," Gigi said, laughing.

"I am!" I responded, as the tears welled up. And then I dumped it all on my dear friend. Everything I wrote about here with much more detail and many more tears. I unloaded it all into her ears.

I will not share her exact words, other than to tell you she patiently and prayerfully led me into the presence of Jesus so that I could focus on Him and entrust to Him the burdens I was never meant to carry.

In those moments, absolutely nothing changed around me, and yet everything changed within me.

I found *peace*.

> "You will keep in perfect peace all who trust in you, all whose thoughts are fixed on you!"
>
> (Isaiah 26:3 NLT)

So, come to the end of yourself. And when you do, prayerfully focus your mind on the Lord instead of whatever obstacles you and your loved ones are facing. He'll supernaturally provide a peace that doesn't even make sense. And if, like me, you need some peace-seeking help, call a trusted friend with listening ears and a warm, Jesus-filled heart. You'll be glad you did.

Day 36

Lord, I Need a Reset

Pamela Christian

"Forget the former things; do not dwell on the past. See,
I am doing a new thing! Now it springs up; do you not
perceive it? I am making a way in the wilderness and
streams in the wasteland."

(Isaiah 43:18-19 NIV)

Sitting at my desk in my office in April 2019, I broke down in front
of my computer. The pain of more than two decades had finally
overtaken my ability to rise above the heartache.

One person very important to me had entirely broken trust. Another, who'd been a very close friend for many years, suddenly and
with no indicators, severed our relationship. A few others in the
workplace, influenced by outright lies of the enemy, had made sadly wrong assumptions about me.

With the Lord's help, I'd been able to overcome the ongoing pain
and loss, knowing I was innocent in each of these matters. I chose
to trust God to right all wrongs. But this day had brought fresh
rejection and false accusations, and I had reached my limit.

"Lord, it's been years since most of these matters originated. I have
yet to be vindicated. You know how I've prayed for those who have

wronged me, wanting them to come to the truth. I've asked for a genuine restoration in my relationships with them. Now I just can't continue being weighed down with this any longer. I need a system reset!"

Staring at my computer, I was suddenly reminded of the many times it needed to be restored to an earlier date in order to function properly. I wished God would restore me to a date after the original hurtful events, so I could be refreshed and move forward without the heavy emotional load. I knew I'd fully forgiven them. There was no bitterness on my part. Just a deep sadness for the continuation of the unrecognized truth that could restore individuals and relationships.

"Lord, what year do You want to restore me to?" It seemed so clear He said "2012." I thought, *2012, what was I doing that year? That was a good year and well after the original painful events. My daughter's wedding was that year ... I was unexpectedly cast in a national television commercial which was fun ... I'd begun efforts to write a book—something I never thought I would do—which turned into a full series over the years.*

"Yeah, 2012, I like that idea, Lord!"

Once I embraced the idea, I was reminded by the Holy Spirit that 2012 was seven years ago. God sometimes works in cycles of seven, which could mean that day was the beginning of a new seven-year cycle. The hope before me loomed large, and I felt a peace come over my heart and soul I hadn't enjoyed in a long time.

Since that day, whenever the pain of past hurts seeks to burden me, I declare, "Nope, I have had a system reset. Anything prior to 2012 no longer has a hold on me." I recall the promise of Isaiah 43:18-19, re-embrace my new beginning, and move forward with peace of heart, mind and soul—all with assurance that God will right all wrongs.

Unforgiveness and bitterness are two things that can hinder any relationship. Knowing this, I've worked hard with the help of the Holy Spirit to prevent that kind of hardening of my heart. I'm guided and inspired by the story of Job: "After Job had prayed for his friends, the LORD restored his fortunes and gave him twice as much as he had before" (Job 42:10 NIV).

Jesus instructed us to forgive seventy times seven (Matthew 18:22). Ever-forgiving others keeps the door of restoration with others open. It also keeps me close to God's heart, as He has continually shown undeserved forgiveness to me.

Thank You Jesus, for giving me the peace my heart sorely needed.

Day 37

When He Calms Our Heart

Janet Eckles

"Have I not commanded you? Be strong and courageous.
Do not be terrified; do not be discouraged, for the Lord
your God will be with you wherever you go."

(Joshua 1:9 NIV)

"I can't take it anymore," my friend said. "The bad stuff in the news that never ends is making me crazy." Did you ever feel that way? Many do. To make it worse, we have to add our personal problems to the mess. Before you know it, stress rises like the temperature in Orlando's summer.

But no matter what heat of adversity burns our peace, none are a match to God's abilities, His power and strength.

I learned that firsthand when at 31, a retinal disease robbed me of my eyesight completely. But the darkness that surrounded me didn't compare to the light He shone in my life. That's because I compared the devastation to His divine ability to usher me to victory, to guide my steps. To use me so others could see Him more clearly.

"Wouldn't you consider eye surgery to see again?" A friend asked. I thought about it for a while. Years ago, I would have done anything at all to regain even the ability to see shadows. But things had changed. "I'll have to think about that," I said.

She chuckled. "Oh no! If you get your sight back, you'll see all my wrinkles. Ugh."

"Stop it. All my friends are beautiful. I see their heart and who they are inside. That's the great thing about being blind."

Blindness, cancer, tragedies, war, and setbacks all happen. But God also happens ... to be greater than any circumstance and can bring solutions to any problem. He is more than capable to heal any pain. And more aware of the details than we could ever be.

So why not release these problems to Him?

Because we're stubborn and we hold on tight to issues that don't belong to us.

Joshua was tempted to do the same. When he faced the transition from following Moses to becoming the leader of God's people, he secretly held on to his insecurities at night. I wonder if during the day he was taunted by feeling alone in the journey.

We do the same when an uncomfortable challenge rattles our peace. We ask: *Do I have what it takes? Am I prepared? Will I be strong enough?*

Those same questions likely stressed Joshua, too. That's why God spoke with emphatic assurance: "Have I not commanded you? Be strong and courageous. Do not be terrified; do not be discouraged, for the Lord your God will be with you wherever you go" (Joshua 1:9 NIV).

God's order was clear then, and it's clear now. *Don't be discouraged, don't fear or worry.* And then comes the promise: *God will be with us.* In the unknown, God will be there. In the uncertainty, He will be there. Even while changes unfold, God will be with us. When stepping into strange territory, God will be there too.

In the tough times, hard roads, and painful days God will be there. Jesus assured His disciples of that: "I have told you these things, so that in me you may have peace. In this world you will have trouble. But take heart! I have overcome the world" (John 16:33 NIV).

Friend, He overcame the world. He overcame the illness that holds you down, the heartache that robs your sleep, and the uncertainty that keeps you fretting.

It's our freedom that Jesus came for. It's for our eternal security He died. And it's for our peace and comfort that He lives again. And because He does, in the midst of the pain the world dishes out, He pours out grace, calms our heart, and fills it with peace.

Day 38

Peacekeeping Forces

Anita Renfroe

"You will keep in perfect peace those whose minds are steadfast, because they trust in you"

(Isaiah 26:3 NIV).

OK. I'm just gonna put this out there:

I don't believe traffic circles belong in America.

They remind me of my very terrible tries at running into an already-moving jump rope being held by two friends in elementary school. I never quite got the rhythm of when to jump in and usually ended up with jump rope resting between my shoulders and the ground. *Wonkwonkwonk.* And it's not that traffic circles aren't a good idea for other places around the globe, it's just overly complicated for people who have had years of green/yellow/red and stop sign indoctrination. Give me a good ol' stop sign any ol' day. I'll even take the awkward "whose turn is it?" glances we endure at a four-way stop. Because it's simple.

I like simple.

I like easy.

I like uncomplicated.

And I wish life worked like that—simple, easy, uncomplicated.

I have experienced a few moments of simplicity and ease in my life. I believe they were when I was between the ages of four to six years old. I only recognize them as airy wisps of memory, before the skinny girls doubled up on the teeter-totter to hold the "husky" girl suspended in midair until they both jumped off and sent me hurtling down to the playground dirt in humiliation.

So young for the disruption of my peace.

I bet you can find an early event that signaled the beginning of the idea that peace was disrupt-able, disturb-able. This broken world always has a way of letting us know in no uncertain terms that life will be complicated and difficult. You know—the opposite of easy.

If you are a Jesus follower, you can probably just as surely recall when you felt the sweetness of deciding to give your complicated, messy life to Him and an immediate peace that came with that decision. What a beautiful gift His peace is in our lives. He even told His followers that it was (in the words of famous game show hosts) a lovely parting gift: He would leave His peace with us, an otherworldly peace. In John 14:27 Jesus tells us this is our secret weapon against worry and fear.

I have many times imagined that the peace Jesus was talking about should just come to me as my divine birthright, preferably as a cooing dove or monarch butterfly and alight upon my forearm and impart a feeling of deep and utter spiritual and emotional bliss with absolutely no effort on my part.

Woohoo! That should just about handle it, right? Right?

Nope, nope, and more nope.

There's a really good reason for the dissonance we feel between what Jesus is saying and how we experience peace precisely because it's not easy. It's because peace requires both a battle and surrender at the same time.

We've all intersected with Reinhold Neihbur's Serenity Prayer and could probably even quote it from memory:

> God, grant me the serenity to accept the things I cannot change,
>
> The courage to change those things that I can change,
>
> And the wisdom to know the difference.

This prayer shows us both the battle (courage to face change) and the surrender (accept the unalterable). Peace comes to us as a gift, and also with some interior work attached.

1. Peace must be desired. Hey, we all know people who are usually looking to stir the pot, people who love a dust up. They might make all the right noises about wanting more peace but live for the adrenal rush of confrontation. Maybe a moment of introspection with your heart to identify your level of desire for peace might be appropriate here. In short: how bad do ya want it?

2. Peace must be received. Like any gift, it's only yours if you take it. We must believe it exists, that Jesus is not trying to hide it from us, and we can make the conscious decision to receive it daily from Him.

3. Peace must be kept. The military term "peacekeeping mission" usually occurs in an area overrun with generations of war, and the United Nations troops are attempting to establish order. When Ben Franklin was asked after the Continental Congress, "Sir, what form of government are we to have?" He replied, "A republic, ma'am, if you can keep it." In the same way, what good is a gift of peace if we aren't interested in doing the work of keeping it? Am I my own peacekeeper? Do I feed my soul Scripture, my mind lovely thoughts? Or

do I allow the negative loops of my past to occupy my emotional real estate day in, day out? Do I limit my exposure to strive-y people? Peace is worth defending.

4. Peace requires surrender. Some people believe the secret to a peaceful life is to live in denial of reality. They prefer to ignore the mountain of baggage building up under their emotional rug. (I may have mixed a metaphor or two, but you get the picture.) This kind of surrender recognizes some things in your life will probably not get solved this side of heaven. I know this is a hard one to wrestle down. We pray. We seek counseling. We want to understand. *We want it to get resolved like a network crime procedural in 42 minutes, dog gone it.* And it doesn't. And we live with the low-grade fever called "disappointment with God" and wonder why we can't find peace anymore. Maybe you can't go back and hash it out with people who are no longer alive. And, even if you could, there's no guarantee that they would give you the magic conversation you have dreamed of having—the one that suddenly explains it all, gives insight into their decisions, makes you feel loved and whole again. Some things just won't get solved this side of heaven. Surrender. Into the aching void Jesus wants to give you His peace.

5. Peace needs intentional focus on the giver. In Isaiah 26:3 there is a promise that God will keep us in "perfect peace" and it carries only one stipulation: that we keep our mind intentionally focused on Him. "But Lord! Have you even seen what's going on down here lately? Are you aware of my current circumstances? Have you seen my stack of bills? My kids' report cards? My to-do list? My cuticles?" Breathe. Focus your thoughts on Him. Breathe.

It's neither easy nor uncomplicated, but it's worth it. It's a battle *and* surrender. Girl: keep your peace.

Day 39

Peace in Sudden Change

Lilian de Silva

"I am the LORD, the God of all mankind. Is anything
too hard for me?"

(Jeremiah 32:27 NIV)

It was a lovely Thursday evening. I had watered the flowers in my garden, finished with my afternoon chores, washed up and dressed for the evening. This time of day my husband and I would sit together singing praise songs and remembering all the times in our lives through which the Lord had taken us.

In addition to these thankful thoughts, I had concerns, too. For two years I had been caring for my husband after a fracture that kept him dependent on a walker. I kept him clean and fresh. I cared for all his needs. We were always together. We understood that season was from the Lord, a time to rest in His presence and to be happy together. Gradually he had progressed to the point I could not leave him and go anywhere.

This particular evening turned out to be different. As we were seated there, my vision suddenly darkened. We didn't know it, but I was experiencing the first symptom of a massive heart attack. The next day, my doctor ordered me to the hospital for immediate treatment. With no prior arrangements, I had to leave my husband and go. If we had known and considered the changes, we could have prepared. This caught us completely off-guard.

How could I stay days in the hospital? We had made no plans for my duties to be taken over. But the Lord had a plan for our situation.

I had no time to think, only to go. As I asked my daughter-in-law (who was there) to give dinner to my husband, the phone rang. It was my daughter calling to tell me they were coming to bring Dad home with them.

As He always has, the Lord had provided. And peace flooded my heart to see how He managed the situation—even without me carefully making plans. Nothing takes God by surprise. He has everything in hand, and we can trust Him, even when everything suddenly changes. When we unload our burdens, put them at His feet, He will provide the solution.

Jesus said, "With men this is impossible; but with God all things are possible" (Matthew 19:26 KJV). We can be at peace no matter what happens.

We often can make it harder to trust by clinging to our own hurried plans. It is our instinct to take the burden for our well-being onto our own shoulders. So in His grace, He takes us through times when He gently demonstrates He can and will handle what comes at us. I know in my case, He had used many lesser problems to teach me to trust Him before that critical moment one Thursday evening. After years of seeing Him prove Himself over and over, I could be at peace during a terrible crisis.

It is not natural to trust God easily. It is a learning process for us to receive the peace Jesus provides. Lean in to what God is teaching you today. You may find yourself grateful someday when everything around you falls apart.

Day 40

How is My Peace?

Lori Altebaumer

"Peace I leave with you; My peace I give to you; not as the world gives do I give to you. Let not your heart be troubled, neither let it be afraid."

(John 14:27 NKJV)

We were visiting Israel during a time of heightened tension. Hundreds of rockets from across the border were being launched into the country. Most were intercepted by the Israeli air defense system, known as the Iron Dome, and while there were a few heart-breaking fatalities, it seemed little other damage was being done.

During this time, the most fear and concern we felt came from our friends back in the States. Had they not sent multiple text messages asking if we were okay, we might not have known anything out of the ordinary was occurring.

Maybe because, to the Israeli people, it wasn't out of the ordinary. It was life as usual. A member of our group asked our guide how the Israelis felt about this. Were they concerned? His answer: "For Israel, this is peace."

His words, softly spoken as a simple matter of fact, shouted truth to our group of pilgrims who would never view peace the same again. In the history of Israel, there has never been a time when they were truly at peace. At least not in the worldly definition of the word.

And yet, from their language and culture comes one of the most beautiful and life-giving words to be spoken in any language. *Shalom.* The word means peace, but so much more.

In Israel, they have learned what it means to have the peace that passes understanding. For the Christian, that gift has been given to us by Jesus Christ Himself.

The peace of *shalom* is not an absence of trouble. It is the peace that comes from understanding that in Christ we have received every spiritual blessing. It is a word that implies the completeness or wholeness that comes from resting in the promises of God.

In the verse above, Jesus tells us not to look for a peace the world can give. Any peace we find that is from this world will be fleeting. We have only to look at history to know when one worry is eliminated, something else will come to take its place. Jesus alone offers peace that lasts. The riches of His glorious inheritance are ours to share. Nothing the world can do can take that inheritance from us, and nothing the world offers can compare to the joy this should give us.

In belonging to Christ, we need not fear the present or the future. Having the peace of Christ won't rid the world of trouble. Instead, it gives us new eyes through which to see the world. Until we can look at life through the lens of this peace, nothing else will comfort or satisfy us.

No matter how many other blessings we are given—health, wealth, a good job, a big house, or a beautiful family—without peace we can never enjoy them. And if we are waiting on the world to give us peace, we are wasting our time and a pursuing a false hope.

The Jewish people have a greeting in Israel, *"Ma shlomcha?"* It is a variation of the word *shalom,* and it means, "How is your peace?"

Not: How is your job? How is your family? How is your health?

But, how is your peace—your shalom?

How am I letting the peace that Christ has given me shape my day? Are my choices and decisions being influenced properly by my shalom? My relationships? My attitude? How different our days—and nights—might look if we asked ourselves this question often.

Ma shlomcha? How is your peace?

Day 41

To Ride Again

Dianne Butts

"May the God of hope fill you with all joy and peace as you trust in him, so that you may overflow with hope by the power of the Holy Spirit."

(Romans 15:13 NIV)

One Saturday in June 2013, I swung my leg over the seat of my burgundy Kawasaki motorcycle and pressed the starter. I buckled my helmet, then followed my husband's Harley out of the drive-way. We met our friend, Margi, and headed up the highway. Hal led, I followed, and Margi brought up the rear on her red 2009 Yamaha. I really liked Margi's bike, with the exception of its color.

Displaying Christian patches on our vests, we prayed with many riders throughout the lovely day. But the trip back was a different story. At 75 miles-per-hour, my tire blew, and I immediately lost my ability to steer. I was thrown off and sent tumbling down the highway.

My injuries were significant. I had large patches of road-rash on my arms, a chipped bone in my ankle, and needed stitches in an elbow. But my helmet had saved my life. The Kawasaki was totaled.

The road-rash would take a year to heal. During that time, I wondered: should I buy another motorcycle or hang up my helmet? I'd enjoyed riding since I was old enough to get a license. My desire was to ride again, but I needed God's peace before jumping back into riding solo. I prayed for guidance I might recognize.

God promised Jeremiah that "You will seek me and find me when you seek me with all your heart" (Jeremiah 29:13 NIV). Jesus also assured His disciples: "Ask and it will be given to you; seek and you will find; knock and the door will be opened to you" (Matthew 7:7 NIV).

God communicates in all sorts of ways when people seek His wisdom. He communicated to Moses specific instructions to build the Tabernacle and to David the building plans for the temple. He answered Gideon's concerns with a fleece. He instructed Mary through an angel and guided her fiancé, Joseph, through two different dreams. I knew He could communicate with me, too. I just didn't know how He would do it. So I watched and waited.

After the accident, Hal, Margi, and I decided to retake our unfinished trip when I had healed enough to ride with Hal. Fourteen months later, I climbed on the back seat of Hal's Harley, and down the highway we went. On a whim, I asked that we stop at a motorcycle shop not far off our route, just to see what bikes they had. I was not planning to buy anything.

We ambled up rows of used motorcycles. That's when I saw one the identical twin to Margi's: a 2009 Yamaha. The exact year and model. The previous owner had added the same saddlebags and windshield. Remarkably, it only had 499 miles. And it was in my price range.

There I stood with the two people I'd ridden with the day I crashed, repeating the same ride, and looking at a clone of Margi's red motorcycle, except it was blue. The bike shop had just gotten it in. It would sell quickly. I needed to decide if I wanted to buy it.

This wonderful gift from God couldn't have been clearer. We knew God had orchestrated all those "coincidences" to communicate His

142

will for me that day. Feeling the Lord had placed this particular bike at this particular place, at that particular time, Hal and I made the purchase.

Though anxiety tickled my insides, peace about riding again filled my heart and mind. I rode that bike home with the Lord's peace, and I'm still riding with it today.

Day 42

Peaceful Landings

Peggy Cunningham

"You will keep him in perfect peace, whose mind is
stayed on You: because he trusts in You."

(Isaiah 26:3 NKJV)

Do you like to fly? I can't imagine looking forward to any day I
have to board a plane, even though I know at the end of my flight,
I'll be home in the USA. I never look forward to squeezing myself
into a small, uncomfortable seat to endure many hours of international flights. And let's not forget turbulence. I'd rather have a root
canal.

Of course, we've all heard that landings and take-offs are the
most dangerous parts of the flight, while soaring through the air
at 30,000 feet is the safest. Does that information comfort you?
Not me. On landings and take-offs, my knuckles turn white from
clutching the armrests, and my heart reaches the rate of a marathon
runner about to cross the finish line.

I once drove to the airport with a physics teacher. She explained
all the aerodynamics of flying. I could have understood her explanation easier if she had spoken in Chinese—and I don't speak

Chinese. "Flying is the safest means of transportation," she told me. Did I feel safer boarding after that conversation? Not. A. Bit.

So, how can we board a plane without our stomachs turning flip-flops over potential turbulence ahead? More importantly, once we arrive, how can we peacefully navigate through the other frightening circumstances in our lives?

I found the answer while descending from 30,000 feet.

A few years ago, my husband and I were each scheduled for surgery in the States. My cataracts were seriously impairing my vision, and my husband had lived the past three years with nerve pain in his back. Weeks before our flight, God had clearly guided us to the right doctors at the right time for both of us. We soared through the heavens (flying again) on our way to our first appointments a few days later.

As we descended to our first destination, I chatted with my husband about the events of the last few weeks. We praised God together for answered prayers and the hope we both had—life without pain for him and good vision for me. God had faithfully orchestrated our plans for good, demonstrating His love and faithfulness to us.

My heart rejoiced as I recounted His answers to our prayers. In those moments, my mind overflowed with thoughts of Him. Suddenly, I was startled to feel the wheels of the plane touch the ground. I hadn't even noticed we were descending until I felt the bump of the landing. I was shocked that my fears of the landing had vanished as I praised God and fully kept my mind on Him.

I know there will be sad and even frightening circumstances ahead. But when they come, I'll recount the day of the peaceful landing and remember to fix my mind on Him, not on my circumstances.

How about you? Are you peacefully gliding or turbulently bumping today? If you're like me, bumpy comes often. Do you wonder how or where you'll land after the bumps? I found the answer for my proverbial peaceful landings. Have you?

Day 43

Peace in Crisis

Debb Hackett

"Even though I walk through the valley of the shadow of death, I will fear no evil, for you are with me; your rod and your staff, they comfort me."

(Psalm 23:4 NIV)

If I could choose a superpower, it would be peace.

My husband is a military test pilot, and before that, was a fighter pilot. I still remember the call from a well-meaning friend one morning while I was at work. He was about two months into his second deployment of our relationship, and I was surviving emotionally by writing every day, sending packages twice a week, and checking the days until his return off the calendar.

"Hey Debb, I just heard from a friend who works at Willy's base. There was a signal from the ship about an incident with his jet. Just checking that he's okay."

The world lurched, taking my sense of wellbeing to a galaxy far, far away. What followed next would teach me a valuable lesson. First, I cried, hot, ugly tears of terror, next I freaked out while still crying, and then I got on the phone with another pilot who worked at the base and wasn't part of the deployment.

Finally, when I had done everything I could in my strength, I remembered to pray. Not the calm, assured prayers of the mature Christian I should've been after fifteen years. Nope. The panicked, breathless, "I'll promise You anything, Lord" prayers of someone who had more fear than faith.

Just minutes later, our friend called and explained what had happened and that all was well.

Since then, I have spent significant time in my Bible. I also lost two members of my immediate family and suffered a miscarriage. Each time I could turn to prayer instead of panic.

God hadn't changed, but my experience with His love had.

His presence remained discernable during my darkest moments. I knew I had not been left alone in my sorrow for a single second. Yes, I have grieved bitterly and wept from the very bottom of my soul, but I haven't had to look for the Lord. He walked beside me into those places, going behind and before.

In Psalm 23, we learn we can always have peace because the Lord never leaves us. As David walked through the valley, God was his comfort. There is nothing more peaceful than knowing we are never alone.

David calls the time of trouble "the valley of the shadow of death." This reveals why David is not afraid: *shadows need light to create them*. So even in the darkest moments, the Light of the World is there. He carries His rod and His staff, symbols of ruling and tending.

We serve a good shepherd, also known as the Prince of Peace. As Jesus said, "My sheep hear my voice, and I know them, and they follow Me; and I give eternal life to them, and they will never perish; and no one will snatch them out of My hand" John 10:27-28 NASB).

Day 44

Jesus' Peace is Far Superior

Karen Porter

"Then you will experience God's peace, which exceeds anything we can understand. His peace will guard your hearts and minds as you live in Christ Jesus"

(Philippians 4:7 NLT).

I dreamed I was on a plane going to a tropical paradise. Palm trees, white beaches, island breezes, and days of sit-in-the-sun relaxation. I'd packed flowing gauzy clothes in bright colors of sunshine and tropical fruit. My dream vacation.

When the plane descended for landing, I glanced out, shocked to see snow everywhere. Then the flight attendant announced we would soon land in Switzerland.

I had two choices. I could weep and complain the airline had taken me to the wrong place. I could whine about the cold and moan because I wanted sand and beach. Or I could get off the plane, head to the nearest shop, buy coats and ski clothes, and head for the Alps.

The first choice is full of stress and misery. And regret. The second choice brims with opportunity and adventure. And peace.

Conventional wisdom says if you want peace, change your attitude. The advice is true on the surface. When I stop complaining, my feelings toward trouble change. But Jesus' peace is far superior to how I feel about my trouble. Jesus said, "I am leaving you with a gift—peace of mind and heart. And the peace I give is a gift the world cannot give. So don't be troubled or afraid" (John 14:27 NLT).

His peace is not like the peace our world suggests: change your attitude, smile, be happy, accept your circumstance, run from the pain, work harder, or *carpe diem*. His peace is of the mind and of the heart. Only Jesus has the power to change circumstances, but if He doesn't alter my situation, He still offers peace. "For he Himself is our peace" (Ephesians 2:14 NASB).

Jesus' peace is more than the absence of conflict or war. Jesus' peace is not absence—it is presence. He is our peace.

Once after a full day's work, Jesus sent the disciples across the sea in a boat while He walked up a mountain to pray. A windstorm battered the boat, and they were about to go down, no matter how hard they rowed or how much water they bailed. Just after midnight, Jesus walked to their boat on top of the waves. He said, "Don't be afraid. Take courage! I am here!" (Mark 6:50 NLT). Mark continues, "Then he climbed into the boat, and the wind stopped" (Mark 6:51). Notice the difference His presence makes, "I am here!" When He climbed into the boat—when He was present—peace.

His peace is superior because He not only created the world, He sustains it. As the sustainer, He controls every situation. When it looks bad to me, He is working behind the scenes for my good. (Romans 8:28) Trouble strikes, but He sees and directs the outcome. (Proverbs 19:21) He is faithful and powerful even when solutions seem impossible. (Matthew 19:26).

In his monumental work *The Message*, Eugene Peterson paraphrased it this way.

"Don't fret or worry. Instead of worrying, pray. Let petitions and praises shape your worries into prayers, letting God know your concerns. Before you know it, *a sense of God's wholeness, everything coming together for good,* will come and settle you down. It's wonderful what happens when Christ displaces worry at the center of your life"

(Philippians 4:6-7 THE MESSAGE emphasis mine).

Jesus' far superior peace brings a "sense of wholeness and a feeling of everything coming together for good." What could be better!

Day 45

Welcome to the Prestigious Not Yet Club

Dianne Barker

"Now faith is being sure of what we hope for and certain of what we do not see."

(Hebrews 11:1 NIV)

During a recent conversation with the Lord about unfulfilled promises, I reminded Him of a few things He hasn't done. But I added, "Not yet," so He'd know I still trusted Him.

Unexpectedly, those words satisfied my complaining heart.

When God makes a promise, it's a done deal. He will do it. If it hasn't happened yet, that means I'm just getting closer. There's also the possibility it won't happen in my earthly lifetime, but I have assurance it will happen.

Hebrews 11:1-2 opens with this amazing definition of faith: "Now faith is being sure of what we hope for and certain of what we do not see. This is what the ancients were commended for" (NIV). Next, the writer introduces ordinary people God chose for a special role in His mighty plan: Abel, Enoch, Noah, Abraham, Sarah, Isaac, and Jacob.

"All these people were still living in faith when they died. They did not receive the things promised, they only saw them and welcomed them from a distance..."

(Hebrews 1:13 NIV)

These faith heroes of old belonged to a prestigious organization: the "Not Yet Club." Didn't I see your name on the membership roster? I'm honored to be a member of the "Not Yet Club," hobnobbing with distinguished folks who received promises, then awaited fulfillment.

This wasn't my first conversation with the Lord about promises on hold. Once, tired of waiting, I vented my frustration over the delay. God responded: "I didn't say when." Did He come through? Yes!

Another time, I mentioned how long I'd waited and grumbled that years were slipping by. "We're running out of time. Do You know how old I'll be next birthday?" He said, "As a matter of fact, I know exactly how old you are." Did He come through? Yes!

Later in Hebrews 11, Moses shows up. We learn that in difficult circumstances, "he persevered because he saw him who is invisible" (Hebrews 11:27 NIV).

Focus determines peace. Moses persevered, keeping a forward focus, trusting the promise of God. That's where I find peace—the promise of God.

Remember: when God makes a promise, it's a done deal. He always comes through.

Are you waiting? Be encouraged by people who waited, surrounded by peace. Moses on the journey with God's people to the land of promise. Joseph in prison. Daniel in the lion's den. Shadrach, Meshach, and Abednego in the furnace.

The Hebrews writer ends with a long list of people who held onto peace during uncertainty. My name doesn't qualify for a place next to Abraham, who waited twenty-five years for the son God promised. God came through...then asked him to sacrifice that son on an altar! Unthinkable! But he prepared the altar and raised the knife to slay the boy.

> "By faith Abraham, when God tested him, offered Isaac
> as a sacrifice. He who had received the promises was
> about to sacrifice his one and only son, even though
> God had said to him, 'It is through Isaac that your
> offspring will be reckoned.' Abraham reasoned that God
> could raise the dead, and figuratively speaking, he did
> receive Isaac back from death"
>
> (Hebrews 11:17-18 NIV).

God intervened, providing a lamb to sacrifice.

Circumstances needn't disturb our peace. They are rich soil where faith grows, leading us to trust God, transforming anxiety to peace.

> "You will keep in perfect peace those whose
> minds are steadfast, because they trust in you.
> Trust in the LORD forever, for the LORD, the Lord
> himself, is the Rock eternal"
>
> (Isaiah 26:3-4 NIV).

Keep your gaze on Him who is invisible. Spend your days in the "Not Yet Club" enjoying His peace.

Day 46

Seek Peace in Your Captivity

Donna Nabors

"Seek the peace of the city where I have caused you to
be carried away captive, and pray to the Lord for it; for
in its peace you will have peace."

(Jeremiah 29:7 NKJV)

The tornado sirens blared, and I began pulling things out of the
closet under the stairs. The experts always say an interior room on
the first floor with no windows is the safest place to be. Our closet
in the middle of the house would be the safest place if the tornado
came our way. At 3:00 in the afternoon, it was dark as night, but
we could hear the winds. When the lightening flashed, we could
see the trees bending sideways. So, into the closet we went. After
several minutes huddled under the stairs, the sirens stopped and
the howling winds passed by. Peace.

Living in Texas, this was not the first time I sat in a closet waiting
for a storm to pass. But this day brought me back to a passage I
had read that morning in Jeremiah. While the storm raged outside,
I sought peace in the closet. Once the storm passed, I was free to
return to life as normal.

Israel was under Babylonian rule by King Nebuchadnezzar. False prophets had been telling the people not to submit to the king of Babylon. Then the prophet Jeremiah sent a letter to those carried away into captivity, giving them truth from God.

God told them to build houses, to dwell in them, to plant gardens, and to raise their families. Then He told them to seek the peace of the city where they were held captive, for in that city's peace they would have peace. He promised them they would return home, but not until after seventy years.

It was in our closet under the stairs that God spoke to me about seeking peace where I am found until God says move.

Many times, I have prayed for God to remove a circumstance in my life, but His plan might be for me to find peace within that circumstance for a time. I should pray for peace in the circumstance, not always for removal from that circumstance.

God had a timetable for Israel. It was seventy years. He had a plan. Verse 12 says, "'Then you will call upon Me and go and pray to Me, and I will listen to you. And you will seek Me and find Me, when you search for Me with all your heart. I will be found by you,' says the Lord, and I will bring you back from your captivity" (NKJV).

But not a moment too soon.

I have learned, when finding myself captive in my circumstances, to focus on God and His words. I pray for peace, and in God's timing He brings me home. But not a moment too soon. I continue to seek Him and search for Him with all my heart, and I have found that He can still give peace during the tough times. Circumstances don't have to disappear to experience His peace.

Paul wrote to believers in Philippians 4:6-7 about making our requests known to God through prayer. Verse 7 says "and the peace of God which surpasses all understanding, will guard your hearts and minds through Christ Jesus" (NKJV).

Let's keep our focus on God in any circumstance we find ourselves in on God, so we might also have peace.

158

Day 47

Rest in His Peace

Deb DeArmond

"When you lie down, you will not be afraid; when you
lie down, your sleep will be sweet."

(Proverbs 3:24 NIV)

It was 2:30 am and my brain refused to shut off.

*Stop the mail. Cancel this month's trash service. Check the batteries in
the alarm system and the motion sensor lights.*

*I forgot about the small group! I need someone to lead while we're away.
I could cancel. Our numbers are lower this summer ... No, that doesn't
feel right. What if I can't find anyone at the last minute?*

*Did Ron make the reservation for boarding the dogs while we're gone?
And are they current on their shots? If not, they won't take them and
our flight leaves at 8:00 am tomorrow morning. Then what will we
do?*

I'd looked forward to this vacation for months, and now it seemed
more trouble than it was worth. I still had to finish packing and
create the emergency contact list for my neighbor. I lay in the dark,
unable to sleep. Each time I crossed something off my mental to-

do list, I thought of three more urgent tasks to add. I could feel panic rising in my throat.

I'm grateful for the peace Jesus brings. Or *can* bring if I let Him. Tonight was not that night.

What is so compelling, so important, it could rob me of His incredible gift of peace?

My husband characterizes these moments as "spinning." A frantic review of details I obsess over when under pressure. He's pragmatic—and helpful. "You can call from the airport in the morning to cancel the trash and stop the mail. Email the contact list to Cindy. She's done this for us several times. The info's the same. Chill. We're on vacation starting tomorrow!"

Like that helped. Another reminder of how little time I had left to get it all done.

Is he right? Have I traded God's gift of peace for the panicky illusion of control? That's a bad deal.

The tyranny of schedules, commitments, kid concerns, and finances are difficult to ignore. And when the house is quiet at night, they all show up like the cast of an old sitcom rerun. When I have (on occasion) determined to set the worries aside and commit them to the Lord, I've felt irresponsible. *I should be doing something.* As though God needed an assist from me.

It's laughable, but not funny. Not at all.

How do we stop the spin? Where can we find rest and peace to quiet our anxious hearts?

Rest and peace are two peas in a pod. It's nearly impossible to find one without the other. We can silence the anxiety and the spin *through rest.* And in His rest, there is peace.

It's counterintuitive to take a break, to release the panic-prone thoughts. When turmoil is present, we obsess about what *to do*, rather than where *to be*. In Him—in His peace—is the safest place *to be*. It requires dumping our to-do lists and slowing down enough to hear Him. As we allow ourselves to rest and sink into Him, He surrounds us with His presence, His comfort, and peace becomes real.

Now that's a good deal!

Day 48

Going to a New Land

Crystal Bowman

"The Lord had said to Abram, 'Go from your country, your people and your father's household to the land I will show you.'"

(Genesis 12:1 NIV)

My husband was excited about the opportunity to work in Florida for a year—but me? Not so much. I was comfortable in our cozy Michigan home we had built less than three years earlier. I like my friends and neighbors, and I was blessed to have both sets of parents living near us as we raised our two little boys. When my husband saw I was less than enthused, he said he would wait to decide. He believed if it was God's will for us to go, we would agree.

The thought of uprooting our young family was overwhelming. Caring for a preschooler and toddler was often more than I could manage on any day. How in the world could I pack up clothes and toys and dishes—and everything else we would need to survive— and move 1,500 miles to where I knew no one?! Besides that, our parents would be devastated and would never support this decision.

Then one February afternoon, as fierce winds snapped tree branches and snow and ice pelted against our windows, a year in Florida suddenly sounded more appealing. Instead of feeling anxious about the decision, I felt calm and peaceful. When my husband walked in the door that evening, I looked at him and said, "I'm ready to go."

"I received another call today," he replied. "They need my answer tomorrow."

We made a list of everything that needed to be accomplished before we could leave, then one-by-one we checked off the items on the list. The biggest hurdle was finding someone we could trust to rent our home, but it was not a big deal to God. My husband ran into a high school friend at a restaurant. His friend sold his home to build a new one, but needed a place to live for a year. Done.

As I packed my belongings, I thought of how God told Abram to move to a land God would show him. Abram didn't question God. He didn't check with his relatives to be sure they were okay with this sudden move. Genesis 12:4 says, "So Abram went as the Lord had told him" (NIV). I believe he folded his tent, gathered his belongings, loaded the camels, and just went. He didn't even know where he was going. At least I knew my destination.

Just as God was with Abram, God was also with us. I can't say it was easy, but I can say I had peace. I believed we were doing what God wanted us to do, and He went before us every step of the way. It was exciting to see how He provided everything we needed in ways we could not have imagined.

Our year in Florida was a time of personal and spiritual growth for my husband and me. God continued to lead us day-by-day as we met new friends, visited churches, and shared the love of Jesus with co-workers. We finally returned to our home a year later, a year wiser, and a year stronger in our faith.

If you believe God is leading you to a new land, a new town, or even a new neighborhood, just go. But go in peace!

Day 49

In the Eye of the Storm

Sharon Wilharm

"Then He arose and rebuked the wind, and said to the
sea, 'Peace, be still!' And the wind ceased and there was
a great calm."

(Mark 4:39 NKJV)

As a child growing up in the Florida panhandle, I loved hurricanes.
My dad worked for the power company, which meant whenever a
storm was heading our way, we'd all pile into his work van and join
the other employee families at the company headquarters.

It was like a giant slumber party. The moms would pack plenty of
junk food to snack on. The kids would bring our favorite books
and games. We'd all carry our sleeping bags, but who had time to
sleep? We were too busy playing. While the storm raged outside,
we calmly munched on cookies and brownies while playing rounds
of Monopoly.

As an adult, I realized hurricanes were not all fun and games, but as
seasoned Floridians, my husband and I weren't too worried when
a tropical storm made its way in our direction. We were miles in-
land in a brand-new house we'd just built. Besides, they were only

predicting it to be a category one at landfall. We've been through much worse. We felt no need to overreact.

As the storm developed in the gulf, I calmly baked cookies while my husband brought in our lawn furniture and secured our daughter's swing set. As the storm approached the shore, we settled in for the duration.

At first, it was no big deal. A little rain. Some mild wind. Nothing we'd not experienced dozens of times before. But soon, the wind and rain intensified. We huddled together in our dark hallway, listening to pounding rain and roaring wind. We second guessed our decision not to evacuate. Would our beautiful home be strong enough to withstand the elements?

Then, just as quickly as it came, the rain stopped. The wind subsided. Complete silence. We peeked out the windows, shocked to see beautiful blue sky. We stepped outside, joining the other neighbors as we all marveled at the perfect calm. It was like an idyllic summer day, not a cloud in the sky. But it only lasted a minute or two. We quickly assessed to see if we'd suffered any damage, then hurried inside before the backlash of the hurricane hit. Fortunately, we knew the backside wouldn't be as powerful as the front of the hurricane. We'd been through the worst. We'd experienced the calm. We could make it through the rest.

That was the last hurricane we braved first hand. After that, we evacuated out of the path of oncoming storms. Eventually, we moved to Tennessee, where we discovered the joys of tornadoes. (But that's a whole other story.)

The disciples were just getting to know Jesus when they experienced a frightening wind storm while out at sea. They bailed and bailed, but could not keep up with the water pouring into the boat. Finally, they woke Jesus, who had somehow remained asleep in the stern. He got up, and with a word, calmed the sea and the winds. Mark tells us the disciples said to each other: "Who then is this, that even the wind and the sea obey Him?" (Mark 4:41 NASB).

They had just learned something new about the Lord: nature itself was subject to His hand. Someone with that kind of power was someone they could trust in any situation.

Though I've not weathered any more hurricanes, I have endured plenty of other kinds of storms in my life. When those storms hit, it's easy to get so overwhelmed by the pounding rain and roaring winds I forget that the God I serve is the maker of the rain and wind.

What about you? Are you going through a storm? We can make it through whatever storms befall us if we remember that peace can come even in the storm. The secret is to keep our eyes on Him.

Day 50

The Ultimate Cover-up

Rebecca Barlow Jordan

"You forgave the guilt of your people–yes, you covered
all their sins."

(Psalm 85:2 NLT)

I never intended for it to be a cover-up. It was only an innocent
mistake.

Several years ago, I returned to my roots–in more ways than one.
Yes, I'm back to brunette again. Actually, the blonde was the result
of a beauty salon mistake a few years prior to that: a dryer, process-
ing gentle highlights, failed to work right.

How to resolve the problem of hair, now with multi-colors? Only
a complete cover-up would do. I liked the result, so I kept it. Do
blondes really have more fun? The only problem was, the cover-up
didn't hold. It took more cover-ups as the roots grew out. The more
cover-up jobs we tried, the blonder I got–and the less "natural" I
looked. More cover-ups are never a permanent solution.

But deciding to go natural has its own problems, too. After so
many cover-up applications, how do you mix the old and the new
without your hair looking ... striped as it grows out? The remedy,

I was told, was yet another cover-up–this time, back to my roots, to the original color. That way, as the gray appears, the hair will look more natural. But covering up the blonde with brunette left reddish hues. Not as natural as I had hoped.

Strange thing about cover-ups. They may work for a little while. Eventually the real colors emerge. However, hair is not the issue here. Most of us have tried a few cover-ups in our lives. I spent several years early on trying to "cover-up" some of my mistakes. Not fun, is it? Eventually, the real colors show through. Under the expert x-ray light of the Holy Spirit, layer upon layer is cut and gradually exposed until the cover-up colors are completely gone.

God has done His own cover-up job for us. And the mistakes we thought would define who we were or how we would live have been completely covered by the blood of Christ. His death gave us new peace and new life, one in which our super-natural colors could flourish. He put an end to any further cover-up attempts on our part.

I've decided on no more future hair coloring cover-ups, even though I agree with Robert Browning, who once said, "My business is not to remake myself, but make the absolute best of what God made." Some of us are simply trying to make the best of what God made.

But I can truly say that hair color has nothing to do with how much enjoyment we find in life. Matthew 23:12 says, *"But if you're content to simply be yourself, your life will count for plenty"* (THE MESSAGE).

The only thing that really matters about this entire conversation is the ultimate cover-up Jesus provided, and whether or not we accept it. And it is tied to a full, enjoyable, and meaningful life: *"I came that they may have and enjoy life, and have it in abundance [to the full, till it overflows]"* (John 10:10 AMP).

With Jesus' divine application, there's no need for any more cover-ups. It's definitely a permanent solution.

Day 51

Best Gift Ever

Vicki Heath

"My peace I give you, not as the world gives. Do not let
your hearts be troubled and do not be afraid"

(John 14:27 NIV).

What is the best, most fabulous, wonderful gift you have ever received? My husband gave me a beautifully wrapped pair of pearl earrings celebrating our anniversary. It was extra special because I lost the first pair. I have received homemade Christmas ornaments from my kids. (Thank you, teachers.) I've received countless dinners from precious church people. These gifts have meant something to me. But by far the best gift I ever received was in 1972, when I received the incomparable gift of salvation through Jesus Christ. That gift changed my life forever. Jesus is the Master Gift Giver. His gifts are never returned or abandoned in a pile of wrapping paper. His gifts are priceless. His gifts have purpose. The gifts we receive in Christ are rich beyond measure.

I need His gift of peace, and nobody does peace like Jesus. "My peace I give you, not as the world gives. Do not let your hearts be troubled and do not be afraid" (John 14:27 NIV). Trouble in the world can rob us of peace. He said, "Do not be afraid." Being unafraid seems almost impossible in the world today. It bids me ask: can fear and peace coexist in a human heart? I think so.

My son and daughter-in-law are serving Him in a troubled and dangerous place in the Middle East. And I have a soon to be born grandchild. What about that baby? These thoughts bring worry. *Lord, give me Your peace.* And He does. I have great peace even though my kids are serving Him in a hard place. But I miss them and have concerns. But their obedience to His call outweighs my worry. I focus on their obedience and not my loss of their company or the danger. That brings me peace.

His peace empowers us to move forward. Perhaps you've had a lapse in your quest for healthy eating. Or you walked away from a commitment. Maybe circumstances became difficult through no fault of your own. You have worries and concerns about your family. What do you do now? You move forward in His gift of peace. You remember His great and precious promise that He is with us and with those we love. He abides with us and in us. There is no place where God is not. That promise brings us peace.

I have experienced trouble in my soul, worrying about the future for my children and grandchildren. This worry troubles my sleep, my relationships, and my peace. When I lean into Jesus, He reminds me of my personal peace gift from Christ Himself. I grab it and hold it close to my troubled heart. I claim out loud and thank Him in my worship. I live it, trusting Him to give me sweet rest and sleep. He is our Peace. Nobody does peace like Jesus.

Day 52

Peaceful as a Weaned Child

Doris Hoover

"But I have stilled and quieted my soul."

(Psalm 131:2 BSB)

A personal issue is making me anxious, so I go for a walk. The moon is a silver crescent gleaming overhead, and the evening sky wraps around me like a deep blue comforter. While others are inside their houses, I'm out walking in the still of the night.

As my feet pound out my stress, a Bible verse comes to mind. "My heart is not proud, O Lord, my eyes are not haughty; I do not concern myself with great matters or things too wonderful for me" (Psalm 131:1 NIV). In the evening stillness, while stars flicker like candles, I look up and pray those words, admitting there are matters I can't control; nor is it my responsibility to do so. I ask the Lord to handle the issue that's disturbing my peace.

With that admission, a weight lifts from my heart.

I remember Who reigns over the earth — and it's not me. It's not my place to solve my complex problems. There are higher thoughts for my mind to dwell on, thoughts more important than the turmoil of my troubles. So beneath a quiet sky, I turn my mind away from my problem to focus on the Lord's majesty above me.

The Lord provides a way for us to hold peace in our hearts. He invites us to focus on His magnificence. When we turn our eyes away from earthly troubles and look toward God, a calmness, as soothing as gentle moonlight, settles over our spirits.

Even David, a mighty warrior and powerful king, turned to God for comfort. When troubles disturbed his peace of mind, he cried out to the Lord. In fact, King David compared the experience of releasing his worries to God as being like a weaned child. "But I have calmed and quietened myself, I am like a weaned child with its mother, like a weaned child I am content" (Psalm 131:2 NIV).

A weaned child differs from a nursing child. A nursing child is restless, demanding sustenance, crying and squirming until his mother suckles him at her breast. A weaned child enjoys the simple pleasure of being close to Mama. In her presence, he's at peace. He leans against his mother's side, delighting in the intimacy of being next to her. As she strokes his sweaty brow and hums, the child relaxes, inhaling his mother's familiar scent and listening to the soft sound of her voice. Resting against her side, feeling the rhythm of his mother's heartbeat, the child calms and anxiety drifts away like vapor in the wind.

This is the picture David paints for us in Psalm 131. It is the scene of a still and quiet child at peace by his mother's side. It shows us what resting in the Lord looks like.

We, too, can exchange anxiety for peace by resting in the Lord's presence. Even though we're no longer children, we can experience the still and quiet contentment of a weaned child. There's a soft, warm place where we can lay our heads while our tensions float away. As we lean into the Lord's tenderness, He strokes our sweaty brows and hums a gentle tune. With each breath, we inhale God's essence.

Our spirits calm, our bodies go limp, and we rest.

In this place of perfect peace, we don't have to concern ourselves with great matters. The One who rules heaven and earth oversees all that concerns us. We need only climb into our Heavenly Father's lap and lay our cares at His feet. In the Lord's presence, we experience the peace of a weaned child resting beside his mother.

That night, beneath the soft glow of moonlight, the Lord reminded me there's a place of perfect peace beside Him.

Day 53

The Secret to Peace

Dianne Neal Matthews

"Let your eyes look straight ahead; fix your
gaze directly before you."

(Proverbs 4:25 NIV)

"Oh, great—just what I need!" I groaned aloud and used my last
ounce of self-control to avoid bearing down on the horn. The light
at the intersection ahead couldn't get any greener. So why wasn't
traffic moving forward instead of creeping ahead an inch at a time?

I was already in a cranky mood, weighed down by all the problems
that threatened to overwhelm me: financial concerns, troubled relationships, age-related physical issues that kept cropping up, and
worries about the future. My life seemed to be out of control; now
the traffic seemed out of control. All I wanted was to run through
my list of errands and get back home. But I couldn't even get back
on the interstate.

Finally, my car edged forward enough to give me a view of the
holdup: a mother duck calmly marching across five lanes of traffic
with four baby ducks in tow who waddled behind her in single
file. The sight mesmerized me. I sat and stared, wondering, "How

can they not be frightened by all the noise and traffic surrounding them in this busy intersection?"

Then I noticed how intently the mother duck was staring at her destination—the other side of the street. As for the ducklings, they kept their eyes fixed straight ahead on Mama. Never looking to the right or left. Never hurrying or running. Simply plodding along on their little webbed feet behind the one they trusted to take care of them, oblivious to the noise and chaos around them on every side.

In that moment God showed me what was missing from my life and the reason it was missing. I lacked peace because I was focusing on my problems and all the things going wrong. I had failed to keep my eyes fixed on Jesus, "the founder and perfecter of our faith" (Hebrews 12:2 ESV). I was looking in the wrong direction.

As Jesus gathered His first disciples to join Him in ministry, He called out, "Follow Me!" He often repeated that phrase as He taught what it means to live a life of faith. In John 10, He compared believers to sheep following their Good Shepherd, trusting Him to keep them safe and meet all their needs so they can find security, rest, and comfort.

Our peace can be stolen by mental turmoil within us or the chaotic culture around us. Watching the news of world events gets more unsettling every day. A multitude of distractions try to pull our eyes off Jesus. It's only by resisting the temptation to let our eyes wander that we can live a life filled with joy, meaning, and peace. Just as we looked to Jesus when we accepted the gift of salvation, victorious living requires us to adjust our eyes continually to keep them focused on Him.

Years have passed since I saw that duck family crossing the busy intersection. But on days when I feel overwhelmed by problems, the crystal-clear image comes back to my mind and inspires me to imitate those baby ducks. I want that same single-minded commitment to keeping my eyes on the One I trust to take care of me and to following Him closely.

Because He has promised not only to bring me safely to my ultimate destination, but to give me peace of mind during the journey there.

Day 54

Pilgrimage to Peace

Nancy Kay Grace

"Blessed are those whose strength is in you, whose
hearts are set on pilgrimage … They go from strength to
strength … "

(Psalm 84:5,7 NIV)

The phone jarred me from a restless afternoon nap. The pain from
stitches in my mouth increased as I struggled to answer the call.
"This is Dr. Bell with the results of your tongue biopsy. I have some
bad news and some good news. The bad news is that it was cancer;
the good news is that we got it all."

My mind froze on the word cancer. I sat at the kitchen table with a
pen and paper, scribbling the date for a consultation appointment.

Cancer. *Tongue* cancer. Never had I imagined this diagnosis. Tears
flowed and fears tumbled together in my soul. A thousand questions flooded my mind. *Where did it come from? What will happen
next? Will I talk clearly again? Why right now, when I feel led to a
speaking ministry?*

I called my husband at work. "Would you come home?" Despair
resounded in my faltering voice. "I *need* you to come home."

We met at the door with a tight embrace as I sobbed. I choked on my words, telling him the news. "We'll get through this, with God's help." He calmed me with the gentle words of a desperate prayer.

A few hours later, I sat at my piano. Music has been my comfort, connecting my heart to the Lord when words fail. My weary soul had no words; I couldn't sing.

I played and prayed through my fingers, lifting every question to God. My heart calmed down as I breathed in His supernatural peace. I knew I would be all right, no matter what happened. I experienced a deeper level of His peace than I'd ever known as I learned to rest in the refuge of God.

God's Word strengthened me on my pilgrimage to recovery. One psalm became precious to me. "Blessed are those whose strength is in you, whose hearts are set on pilgrimage. As they pass through the Valley of Baka, they make it a place of springs; the autumn rains also cover it with pools. They go from strength to strength, till each appears before God in Zion" (Psalm 84:5-7 NIV).

The "Valley of Baka" was known as the *Valley of Weeping*. It was a barren passage pilgrims passed through on the way to Jerusalem. The promise in these verses is that the place of weeping becomes a passage to a "place of springs," or refreshment. My "Valley of Baka" was a place of drawing hope and peace from the Lord.

The Psalmist speaks of going from "strength to strength." The secret is found in the word *to*. While we enjoy the mountaintop experiences of life, in reality, more time is spent living in between the mountaintops, going from strength *to* strength. God restored my heart with greater trust for Him.

When I received my first tongue cancer diagnosis, I had little emotional strength. I leaned into God's faithful and loving nature. His peace comforted me in the upheaval.

The treatment for this tongue cancer was to biopsy any suspicious tissue. The assurance of God's presence and strength has carried me through seven tongue biopsies in 15 years. Twice it was cancerous, each time it was removed early enough that no other treatment was needed. Seven times I've had to relearn how to talk. Each time, the refuge of God led me to peace.

I am so grateful. My desire remains to use my faltering tongue to speak of Jesus, my Prince of Peace.

Day 55

Face to Face with Shalom

Karen DeArmond Gardner

"Then Gideon built an altar there to the LORD and named it The LORD is Peace."

(Judges 6:24 NASB)

I longed for peace, but it seemed as elusive as a butterfly fluttering just out of reach. At the time, I thought peace must mean calm, but calm can also be a precursor to a storm.

To a survivor of trauma, peace seemed unobtainable. I questioned God much like Gideon did: wondering where He was and why I wasn't worthy enough to be rescued.

I escaped my abusive marriage in late 2004. Since then, it has been a healing journey, rediscovering who God is and who He created me to be. Gideon's encounter with the Angel of the Lord parallels my story in many ways. We both endured horrific trauma and saw ourselves as less than we were.

Gideon's story, found in Judges 6:1–24, details Gideon's transformation from mouse to warrior. That was accomplished through his interaction with the Angel of the Lord, who spoke identity and courage into Gideon after he (and his people) had been severely traumatized by Midian.

Gideon doubted the Angel of the Lord's news that he was appointed to rescue Israel from the Midianites. They were a powerful army who had ravaged Israel for years. Gideon asked the Angel to wait while he prepared a meal, which became a burnt offering to God, and then the Angel of the Lord vanished.

Imagine Gideon's shock and surprise when he realized he'd been face to face with the Angel of the Lord and didn't die (vs. 22-23).

"So, Gideon built an altar to the Lord there and called it Yahweh Shalom" (Judges 6:24 NASB). After the encounter, Gideon experienced Shalom, which is so much more than a lack of chaos. Shalom is wellbeing, a wholeness, favor, victory, and the destruction of chaos. It also confirmed for Gideon that he would be the one to lead Israel.

Like Gideon, I desperately needed Shalom in my life.

2019 was a rough year for me emotionally. Since 2004, I'd experienced deep healing, though I never truly acknowledged all I had lost. God used an event in April to trigger ten months of grieving. As I experienced the rollercoaster of grief, I realized I was grieving thirty years of trauma by the one who should have loved me.

I lived in a constant state of chaos and pain until one night, when I lay in my bed sobbing, my words dried up except for repeating: *Jesus.* Part of me knew the Holy Spirit was interceding on my behalf, putting words to my groans (Romans 8:26). I just wanted the pain to stop, so I asked a simple question, "God, what do You want to say to me?"

Shalom.

As the word Shalom settled in my spirit, peace came over me in a way I'd never experienced before. It was the peace Paul describes in Philippians 4:7 (HSCB), "And the peace of God which surpasses every thought, will guard your hearts and minds in Christ Jesus."

Gideon built an altar after his encounter with the Lord. He now had a peace that comes from Yahweh Shalom.

My season of grieving ended in January 2020. The peace the Lord gave me in that season remains with me to this day. The journey through grief has deepened my relationship with the Father, Jesus, and Holy Spirit. My story shifted. Rather than being about what I went through, it is now about what God did with what I went through.

Do you long for healing, wholeness, and victory? Ask Yahweh Shalom for His peace and step into the arms of the Great Healer. He will not disappoint.

Day 56

Mourning Peace

Louise Tucker Jones

"For I will turn their mourning into joy and will comfort them and give them joy for their sorrow. I will fill the soul of the priests with abundance, and My people will be satisfied with My goodness, declares the Lord."

(Jeremiah 31:13-14 NASB)

It had been several sad and lonely weeks since my three-month-old son, Travis, died suddenly from undiagnosed congenital heart disease. In fact, the weeks had now turned into months. The sadness was more than sad, and the grief still so raw it cut my heart in two. The shock of his death brought me to my knees as I held onto God with all of my strength.

But now my heart was so broken I couldn't even pray. Questions assaulted me. Where was God? Why didn't He prevent this? What kind of God takes babies from their mothers? I felt totally abandoned and became so angry I vowed to never pray to God again.

There was just one problem. I had a four-year-old son, Aaron, who missed his brother dearly. He would ask me questions daily. "Mommy, what's Heaven like?" "Mommy, can I go to Heaven and see Travis?" Or, "Mommy, why can't Daddy go get Travis and bring him home?"

These are tough questions to answer, especially when you are mad at God.

I couldn't stand the thought of hurting Aaron with the bitterness that was consuming me. I had taught him every day of his young life that Jesus loved him, and I couldn't bear to destroy that faith. I loved my four-year-old son with all my heart, and seeing him in such grief was more than I could bear. I knew I had to find peace beyond my grief so I could be a good mother to Aaron.

Finally, one night, as I lay alone on my bed in the darkened room, I poured out my heart to God—my anger, bitterness and pain. I prayed, "Lord, I have tried to change but I can't. So if You want me whole again, You will have to do it. But please let me know my baby is okay. Please heal my broken heart so I can be a good mother to Aaron."

Suddenly, the room was filled with an unmistakable peace and I heard God speak to my heart, "Louise, Travis is with me. He's okay. He's with me." Then, to my amazement, I felt the weight of my baby son placed against by breast and I could almost smell his precious baby sweetness and feel his soft hair brush against my cheek.

I couldn't open my eyes as tears streamed across my temples, soaking my hair. I lay absolutely still, allowing God to comfort me in a way I had never known as I continued listening to His gentle whisper: "Travis is okay. He's with me."

How long I lay in the mighty presence of my loving God, I don't know. I only know that when I awoke the next morning, the bitterness and anger were gone. I still missed my son, Travis, terribly. I still had no explanation as to "Why?" But I had had the most intimate encounter with God's healing love and His presence than I had ever experienced in my entire life.

That night I learned that the peace He gives can be a palpable, dis-

188

cernible thing. It could supernaturally bind up a mourning heart and bring life and serenity into even terrible grief.

Day 57

What to Do in The Waiting

Debbie Alsdorf

"Whatever happens, conduct yourselves in a manner
worthy of the gospel of Christ"

(Philippians 1:27 NIV).

The day I was diagnosed with cancer was the day my life felt suspended, my calendar wiped clean and my days filled with waiting for the next test results. I had learned how to trust God in the good times—but the hard and unexpected waiting times often caused me to spiral.

I call this waiting in life, *the meantime.* The meantime is that place in between a problem and a solution—a prayer and its answer. Being that the meantime is part of real life, I decided to quit despising the waiting and learn to live well in the hard places.

I began to sit with Paul in Philippians. Meaning I read it over and over, stopping to consider what He was teaching and where he was coming from. Paul's letter to the church in Philippi was written from prison—yet filled with hope. His circumstances were not good, but he still lived in a good place. This is where the rubber meets the road in our faith life. Do we conduct ourselves positively even when things are affecting us negatively?

Like Paul, some of us are waiting out hard situations.

And, though circumstances are often out of our control, there are a few things we do have control over—our attitude, the direction we take, and where we place our hope. Problems are inevitable, but living overwhelmed is optional. Here are some things to consider in the times of waiting …When bad things happen, God is still in control. God holds us together, even when things are falling apart. God is always at work. He is in the details. Suffering is part of life; God sees our tears. Difficult circumstances can change us, and times of waiting shape us.

There is a plan, even when it looks like there isn't. We can learn to resist fear by remembering God.

As I sat in the words of Paul, I became grateful for how his letter to the church built up to practical instruction that teaches us how to wait. God's Word is our guide for learning how to live well in the meantime. In Philippians we see a call to action:

Rejoice—give thanks in all things.

Remember—the Lord is near.

Resist—fear and anxiety and turn the cares into prayers.

Recall—the times God was faithful in the past and thank Him for who He is

Refocus—turn from the negative and look for anything good and dwell on that

Return—to the teachings of scripture, walking out faith the way those before us did.

"Rejoice in the Lord always. The Lord is near. Do not be anxious about anything, but in everything, by prayer and petition, with thanksgiving, present your request to God. And the peace of God, which transcends all understanding, will guard your hearts and your minds in Christ Jesus. Finally, whatever is true ... whatever is pure, whatever is lovely ... if anything is excellent or praiseworthy think about such things. Whatever you have learned or received or heard from me or seen in me, put it into practice"

(Philippians 4:4-9 NIV).

Paul turned from prison to praise and from frustration to faith. That is what I want to learn to put into practice each time I find myself pressed into hard and waiting on God. These days you might find me praying something like, *Lord, help me turn to You in my times of waiting. When life seems unfair and the days are hard, may I press into You. Remind me of Your love so that we I resist fears and refocus. Draw me near as I recall Your faithfulness in the past and return to You with fresh hope for the future.*

Don't Go Down to Egypt

Linda Rooks

"Woe to those who go down to Egypt for help … but
do not look to the Holy One of Israel."

(Isaiah 31:1 NIV)

As I tossed and turned in bed, a look at the alarm clock revealed it
was it was one o'clock in the morning. Two huge problems loomed
before me the next day. I didn't know how I would solve either.
Restlessly, my mind churned through a myriad of possibilities,
searching for answers. Tired and longing for sleep, I sighed and
again looked at the clock.

One-thirty.

Okay, I thought, *I've been down this road before. I'm going to lie
awake all night worrying and be so tired tomorrow I won't be able to
do what is needed to resolve this situation. I need to go to sleep.*

Then I did what I should have done to begin with. I prayed.

Earlier that morning, I had been reading in Isaiah 30 and 31 about
God's displeasure with Judah when they were being threatened by
the Assyrian army. Instead of trusting God and looking to Him for

guidance, they went down to Egypt to solicit help—which He had told them not to do. Even though He had saved them from their enemies on so many previous occasions and showed them signs and wonders throughout their history, the people went their way seeking help from mere men, who worshipped pagan gods.

Of course, the threat was genuine. The Assyrians were a great and powerful army, and Judah alone had no way of standing against them.

Even though it was thousands of years ago, it wasn't too hard to relate to their dilemma. Earthly problems appear to need earthly solutions—don't they? Spiritual principles don't seem relevant when we need practical answers—right? God is wonderful, but what does He have to do with complicated earthly situations that plague our lives?

Well—everything.

Had Judah used their spiritual eyes, remembering the way God had rescued them in the past and trusting Him to do it again, Isaiah tells us they would have enjoyed God's favor and been saved. Instead, they turned to worldly resources. As a result, both they and the Egyptians came to ruin because the Jewish people relied on themselves instead of God.

As the memory of this Scripture drifted through my thoughts, the words, *"Don't go down to Egypt"* began circling through my head as well. I knew God was speaking to me. "Don't look to worldly solutions," He was saying. "Don't worry about how these things will be resolved. Trust me. I will give you peace."

Don't go down to Egypt.

Another story from the Bible popped into my mind—the story of King Hezekiah. A fierce Assyrian army came against him also and demanded his surrender. But Hezekiah went to God, laid all the facts before Him, and prayed, praising God and acknowledging Him as creator and ruler of all. The next morning, thousands of

Assyrian soldiers were dead before one arrow had been shot into the city. Judah was saved (2 Kings 19: 9–37 NIV).

As I thought about God's promises for those who trust in Him, I prayed and surrendered my problem to God. Gradually, my body relaxed, and before long I drifted off to sleep.

The next morning as I read my devotions, the Lord beautifully reaffirmed to me His message from the night before.

Trust me.

God's peace enveloped me, and throughout the day I continued to surrender the situation to Him in prayer. As a result, God remarkably opened a path through a complicated situation to make it not only workable, but perfect in God's timing, according to His inexplicable plan.

Day 59

Kicking Worry Out of the Way

Cindi McMenamin

"Peace I leave with you; my peace I give you. I do not give to you as the world gives. Do not let your hearts be troubled and do not be afraid."

(John 14:27 NIV)

Is worry the unwelcome guest in your home? Worry can stress you out, damage your family relationships, and ultimately give you an ulcer.

The dangerous thing about worry is that it creeps into our lives gradually and makes its home with us before we notice it's there. It usually enters our front door in the form of two words: *What if?*

> *What if I lose my job?*
>
> *What if I can't pay for this?*
>
> *What if it's not benign?*
>
> *What if my worst fear is realized?*

But you don't have to live with worry anymore. At the root of our "what if" questions and greatest fears is what you and I really believe about God's character. When our minds play through the various what ifs, the question we are really asking is "What if God isn't able?" or "What if God isn't good?" or "What if God can't handle this?"

And that is not an attitude, question, or mindset I want dwelling in my home. And I don't think you do either. So, it's time to kick it out the door.

God's Word tells us: "Don't worry about anything, but in everything, through prayer and petition with thanksgiving, present your requests to God. And the peace of God, which surpasses all understanding, will guard your hearts and minds in Christ Jesus" (Philippians 4:6-7 CSB). As you and I give God all of our what ifs and worries, He can calm our hearts and remind us He is in absolute control. Then His peace comes to dwell with us, instead of those fearful thoughts.

When you and I trust God with what is closest to our hearts, we are saying "You, God, are capable. You are trustworthy. And all my worries and what ifs are in vain." We are also saying to those around us: "I trust God will work this out in your life and mine," modeling trust and faith before them.

Give God your concerns today. By doing so, you'll be kicking worry out of your home and welcoming a new family member: trust.

Day 60

Peace that Passes through the Checkout Lane

Linda Evans Shepherd

"The Lord gives his people strength. The Lord
blesses them with peace"

(Psalm 29:11 NLT).

If you are looking for real peace, you may have to step out of your comfort zone and follow God's lead. That's exactly what happened to me one hot May afternoon in the local all-natural grocery store. I'd dashed inside to grab a couple of items but got caught in a long line at the checkout counter. As I inched toward the cash register, I observed that the faces around me seemed bored, well, all except the face of the very pregnant cashier. She looked up from her checking and announced to the line, "Today's my last day here."

There was something in her tone, an urgency in her eyes that caught my attention. When I finally handed her my protein bars, I asked, "Going on maternity leave?"

She stared at me. "I have to get the tumor out."

Tumor? I looked into her frightened eyes and ventured, "What do you mean?"

"Actually," she informed me as she patted her belly, "I have three tumors and one is the size of a grapefruit. The doctor says they all have to come out—now!"

I pushed aside my shyness and asked, "Could I pray for you?"

"Yes, I would love that," she said.

We stepped to the side of the counter where we continued our conversation in full view of the grocery store patrons. I asked, "May I touch your shoulder?"

"Please do," she said, then whispered, "I'm a Christian too."

I gently placed my hand on her shoulder, and we bowed our heads. As all eyes stared, I prayed for healing, for her, for her baby, and prayed that everything would be okay. I prayed she and her child would be blessed.

A look of relief flooded her face. "Oh, thank you for that," she said.

I handed her my baseball cap, embroidered with the word 'Blessed.'

I told her, "As I prayed, I got an overwhelming feeling that everything was going to be all right. I feel like the Lord wants you to know that you and the baby were going to be fine. In fact, you and your little one *will* be blessed."

Tears of hope filled the young woman's eyes as I encouraged, "Wear this hat and remember that God has blessed you, the both of you."

"I will wear it and remember. I promise," she said.

Months later, I found myself back in the grocery store and asked one worker. "Whatever happened to the pregnant woman who was working here last May. Is she okay?"

The worker grinned, "She is! She's absolutely fine. She had the baby!"

"Is the baby okay?" I asked.

"I just saw them, and that baby is the cutest kid you ever saw. They are so blessed!"

Suddenly, I too felt blessed. It seems God had answered my check-out prayer, and I could feel His joy and peace.

I believe that the Lord Himself brought me to the grocery store that afternoon in May and gave me the strength to push past my shyness to pray for a stranger. As I prayed, God blessed the mom-to-be, her baby, and even me.

What peace we feel we allow God to push us into acts of love!

Day 61

Peace Like a River

Lane Jordan

"For thus says the Lord, 'Behold, I extend peace to her like a river. And the glory of the nations like an overflowing stream; and you shall nurse, you shall be carried upon her hip, and bounced upon her knees.'"

(Isaiah 66:12 ESV)

I just got back from a reunion at my childhood camp. It is my favorite place in all the world. I'm not sure if I love it so much because it's on the top of a beautiful North Georgia mountain, or because the food is so good, the activities stupendous, or just because my memories cannot be daunted.

Either way, I love, love this camp and try to get to the reunion each year. At this year's get-together, we of course sang around the campfire with the standard songs sung every night, ending in a tight friendship circle.

One song we sing is "Peace I ask of Thee, O River." I always think, *How can a river give peace?*

And then I remembered. There are verses about rivers in the Bible!

The river is a metaphor for both boundaries and roadways. In the Scripture above, God is using it as a picture of His peace, constant in its flow, just like a slow-moving river, but also overwhelming in its abundance. Its never-ending movement pictures the care and presence He will always provide.

Isaiah was prophesying to a nation that had turned away from God and His peace. He told them, "Oh, that you had paid attention to my commandments! Then your peace would have been like a river, and your righteousness like the waves of the sea" (Isaiah 48:18 ESV). If we seek other places for our security, we cannot rest in His peace.

We may waver, but our God will never change. He and His peace are always there for us.

I love Romans 8:38-39 (NIV). Paul explicitly says that nothing will *ever* be able to separate us from God's love: "For I am convinced that neither death nor life, neither angels nor demons, neither the present nor the future, nor any powers, neither height nor depth, nor anything else in all creation, will be able to separate us from the love of God that is in Christ Jesus our Lord."

That makes me want to jump for joy! These promises are so rich and so large—how could I ever *not* have peace in my life?

God loves us so very much. And He wants to give us His peace every second of every day until we are finally with Him in His eternal home. Placing our confidence in Him will result in a steady stream of peace. Who wouldn't want that?

Day 62

Peace in the Stress-Pool

Debora Coty

"The Lord gives strength to his people; the Lord blesses
his people with peace."

(Psalm 29:11 NIV)

I'm a landlubber. Yes, I'll admit it—my sea legs are as wobbly as a
newborn colt's. It probably has something to do with my first experience aboard a cruise ship while celebrating our tenth wedding
anniversary.

Did I say *ship?* My bad. It was more like an oversized cork, bobbing
up and down on the turbulent Gulf of Mexico for five days with
ten-foot waves sloshing over the railings as Hurricane Gilbert completely wiped out our destination, Cozumel.

I learned what the inside of a paper bag looked like.

I've never felt so helpless and hopeless. Up and down. Back and
forth. Hour after hour the boat lurched, throwing our equilibrium
completely off. We couldn't stagger down the hall without being
hurled into a handrail. And there was nothing we could do to im-
prove our lot. Medication and shots didn't help; we ran out of sea-
sickness bags after the third day.

It was the most miserable, stressful vacation ever.

After my own maritime experience, the storm that rocked Jesus' boat took on new meaning:

> "And a great windstorm arose, and the waves beat into
> the boat, so that it was already filling. But He [Jesus]
> was in the stern, asleep on a pillow. And they awoke
> Him and said to Him, 'Teacher, do You not care that
> we are perishing?' Then He arose and rebuked the wind,
> and said to the sea, 'Peace, be still!' And the wind ceased
> and there was a great calm"
>
> (Mark 4:37-39 NKJV).

"Peace, be still." Wow. Three simple words that stilled the storm, calmed the winds, and brought peace to those in turmoil. No more retching over the rails, no more floundering about while forces over which you have no control hurl you to and fro.

Just what we hope Jesus will do to the storms in our lives.

Hey, did you notice where Jesus was during the worst of the tempest? He was in the stern, curled up on a pillow, *asleep*. Does that sound like someone panicking about his horrendous situation? Someone fearful or frantic?

Not at all. It sounds like someone who knew the outcome of the storm all along. Someone at complete peace with God and Himself, regardless of His circumstances. Someone whom I aspire to emulate.

But you know, Jesus doesn't always quell the storms of our lives, does He? Sometimes we have to experience the strength of the wind and waves before we can appreciate the peace He brings. And it might not be external peace at all; our outward circumstances might continue to surge all around us, but that doesn't mean He can't bring us internal peace in the midst of the chaos. "The Lord gives strength to his people; the LORD blesses his people with peace" (Psalm 29:11 NIV).

Sometimes Jesus calms the storm; sometimes He calms our hearts.

True, the storms of life can fling us about until we don't know which end is up. We may lose our equilibrium for a while, like I did on my cruise from Hades, and feel as if we'll never get off the ship.

But we can learn, like the psalmist, to "embrace peace—don't let it get away!" (Psalm 34:14 THE MESSAGE).

Yes, if we turn to Jesus in our storms, He'll utter those three little words: *"Peace be still."* This proclamation is our inner tube (and I do mean *inner*) to stay afloat in life's stress-pool.

Day 63

Peace for Our Children

Christina Rose

"All your children will be taught by the Lord, and great
will be their peace."

(Isaiah 54:13 NIV)

As a young mother, I was happy to stay at home with my two little
daughters. After years in a corporate office, it was a joy to spend
time with them at the beach, park, zoo, or whenever else we liked.
I am grateful for those glorious, innocent days. Unfortunately, I
became a single mom during that time, and many sleepless nights
were spent praying. I leaned on God day and night.

I returned to work, and the kids started school. With the news of
school shootings and bullying, I was always anxious for their safety.
One day my five-year-old came home from kindergarten and threw
herself onto her bed, sobbing hysterically, "The kids don't like me,
Mom, the kids don't like me!" The tears and hurt on her face were
unbearable.

The ferocious mama bear in me sprang into action. I knew there
could be other disappointments ahead and declared that no weapon formed against us would prosper. We daily petitioned God for

His grace and favor. Throughout the years, God kept us safe and provided for our needs.

During those years, we loved our old VW bus camper, but it kept breaking down. This was a source of great stress. Finances were tight, but we went shopping anyway and fell in love with an SUV complete with DVD player. I could not afford it. That night the kids and I prayed for a miracle.

After they were asleep, I spent more hours praying for that new car. The next morning at work, I printed out a picture of the car and prayed some more. A few hours later, the owner of the building for which I was the property manager arrived. He offered to lease me a new car as a bonus for my hard work. I handed him the picture of the car we wanted. Within a few weeks, we picked up the car and were on our way to Disneyland.

When the girls left for college, they were swept away by new friends and adventures. At times, I felt they had forgotten all about me, our family, and our faith. One day at church when I asked for prayer for the girls, a friend burst into tears. "Teresa, what is wrong?" I asked.

She responded, "I'm going through the same thing with my son, and I'm worried." We prayed together:

"Yes, captives will be taken from warriors; and plunder retrieved from the fierce; I will contend with those who contend with you; and your children I will save"

(Isaiah 49:25 NIV).

Things turned around for both of us and all is well. I've learned that many young adults who leave home initially may stray a bit, but eventually circle back to their families with appreciation. I have witnessed miracles of kids returning and saved after relentless, steadfast prayer. Impossible situations can change overnight. When I look at my two beautiful, successful scientist daughters, I know I did not do it alone. Persistent prayer is the key to peace for our children. I believe God wants our children to have peace in all areas of their lives. The peace of our children is also our peace, their children's peace and a mighty inheritance from God.

"Their children will be mighty in the land;
the generation of the upright will be blessed."

(Psalm 112:2 NIV)

"For I will pour water on the thirsty land, and streams
on the dry ground; I will pour out my Spirit on your
offspring, and my blessing on your descendants. They
will spring up like grass in a meadow, like poplar trees
by flowing streams."

(Isaiah 44:3-4 NIV)

Day 64

Be Anxious for Nothing

Elaine Helms

"Be anxious for nothing, but in everything by prayer
and supplication with thanksgiving let your requests
be made known to God. And the peace of God, which
surpasses all comprehension, will guard your hearts and
your minds in Christ Jesus."

(Philippians 4:6-7 NASB)

My daddy used to say he thought I would worry if I didn't have
something to worry about! He was a military man about to go over-
seas and I was a daddy's girl. He wanted me to know I could tell
Jesus all the things I usually tell him; so he taught me to sing the
hymn, "What a Friend we have in Jesus." When I got a little older,
he also helped me memorize Philippians 4:6-7.

As an adult, I have gotten better at taking "everything to God in
prayer," but I can still lose my peace if I'm not careful. One time
when I was praying, giving my requests to God, I realized I was
still stewing about my concern. I confessed to God that I was being
anxious, and I wanted to be obedient and *not* be anxious. I asked
for His help. Though I don't think it was audible, He told me to

praise Him through the alphabet, to get to know Him better and to trust Him to handle what I had just prayed about.

I got excited and praised God beginning with the letter A. "Lord, I praise you as Almighty God, You are Adonai, You are the Author and finisher of my faith … " It was all going well until I slipped back into thinking about my concern. Like a tap on the shoulder, God reminded me I was on the letter *D*! It took time, but with practice, I got all the way through the alphabet. The amazing result was a peaceful night's sleep.

What are some things that make us anxious? What we will wear? An unkind comment someone made to or about us? Is it hard to go to sleep at night because of worries about children, husband, or something else?

No matter what is troubling us and causing us to be anxious or worried, Jesus is bigger than our concerns. He loves us so much that He gives us the key to peace in Matthew 6:25-33 (NASB). He says, "Do not be worried about your life, as to what you will eat or what you will drink; nor for your body, as to what you will put on. Is not life more than food and the body more than clothing? … And who of you by being worried can add a single hour to his life? Do not worry then … for your heavenly Father knows that you need all these things. But *seek first His kingdom and His righteousness*, and all these things will be added to you." The key to peace is to seek Him and His purposes first!

So the next time anxiety comes to call, remember the key to peace of mind –

> Take it to the Lord in prayer.
>
> Leave it with Him
>
> Focus your thoughts on praising and worshiping Him.

Now where was I? Oh yes, the letter S. "Lord, I praise You for being my Savior, You are Sovereign, the same yesterday, today and forever. Your name is a strong tower, the righteous run into it and are safe. I love You Lord and thank You for Your peace that passes all my understanding."

Day 65

Navigating Life's Storms in Peace

Grace Fox

" Jesus woke up, he rebuked the wind and said to the waves, 'Silence! Be still!' Suddenly the wind stopped, and there was a great calm. Then he asked them, 'Why are you afraid? Do you still have no faith?'"

(Mark 4:39-40 NLT).

Balmy. That's how the day dawned when my husband and I began our trip home after sailing British Columbia's coastal waters for three blissful days. We'd timed our departure and arrival based on weather reports and tide charts. Everything went well for the first four hours, but then things changed. The wind grew stronger than expected, the waves grew rough, and I grew more than a little anxious.

My husband feels comfortable at the helm of a sailboat because he spent his childhood and teen years enjoying water-related activities. He drove a motorboat for the first time when he was six years old. He developed a sailing program at a Christian camp where we worked for more than a decade. He understands the science behind keels and diesel mechanics, tides, currents, and winds.

I grew up on the Alberta prairies. The nearest body of water was a manmade lake ten miles out of town. I was nearly twenty years old before I stepped into a boat. I rowed it backwards and wondered why it moved so slowly. Four decades later, I'm still in learning mode about all things marine.

My hubby's knowledge and experience help him maintain his cool in the cockpit under adverse conditions. My lack thereof causes me to hang on for dear life, let loose with an occasional shriek, down anti-nausea tablets, and pray that our vessel will stay upright. I've even had a few desperate monologues with God that sounded something like this: "You calmed the sea for the disciples, so do it for me! Now!"

I empathize with the disciples' reaction when waves threatened to sink their boat. Convinced that death was imminent, they woke Jesus with panicked shouts: "Teacher, don't you care that we're going to drown?" (Mark 4:37-38 NLT).

Jesus woke, silenced the storm, and then answered the disciples' question with two questions: "Why are you afraid? Do you still have no faith?"

Jesus already knew the answers, but asking the questions invited the disciples to learn something about themselves: the root cause for their fear was not the storm. It was a lack of understanding Jesus' character. They'd watched Him heal the sick, feed the masses, give sight to the blind and more, but they still didn't "get" who He was. Their limited, inaccurate thoughts about Him translated into doubt about His intent toward them and ultimately, fear.

I realize that expanding my understanding about the mechanics of sailing will help me feel more comfortable in bad weather. The more I get how our boat functions and how wind and currents behave, the more confident I'll feel in adverse conditions. The same holds true in the spiritual realm.

The more we understand God's wisdom, sovereignty, power, and love, the less anxious we feel when the storms of life threaten to

218

topple us. We can better trust His ability to carry us through the tumult. And we can trust His intent toward us is always and only good.

As a mariner-in-the-making, I also realize that trying to learn the mechanics of sailing while in a storm isn't conducive to success. I need to learn in advance, so I'm prepared for the unexpected.

Again, the same is true spiritually. Adversity strikes, often when least expected. Let's prepare ourselves by getting to know God better through spending time in His Word, conversing with Him in prayer, actively using our abilities to serve Him, and participating in a growth group where we study and fellowship with other believers. Understanding who God is equips us to face the storms—not consumed by fear, but embraced with supernatural peace.

Day 66

Peace in Tragedy

Monica Schmelter

"I have told you these things so that in me you may
have peace. In the world you have trouble and suffering
but take courage—I have conquered the world."

(John 16:33 NLT)

When I got the call that my closest friend for eighteen years had
been missing for several hours, I tried to convince myself there
must be some reasonable explanation. Perhaps she hopped in her
car for a short drive to blow off some steam? Maybe her phone was
going straight to voicemail because the battery died. She was so
very responsible, a woman who loved her family and never failed
to communicate her whereabouts. I promised her husband the moment I heard from her I would contact him immediately.

Of course, I prayed. I called and texted our mutual friends. I
reached out on social media. I worried. I cried. I waited for my
phone to ring. Later that afternoon, I received the tragic news: my
best friend had taken her life.

I never saw that coming. I knew she struggled with depression
and anxiety, but when we talked, she said she was doing well, and
counseling was helping immensely.

Her memorial service and the days to follow are still a blur for me. I am not sure when it happened, but at some point, I wondered what I had missed. How did I not know that my dearest friend was suicidal? We talked frequently and texted almost every day. What kind of friend was I, anyway?

Despite my best efforts, I just couldn't understand what went wrong. I prayed. I talked with friends. I sought godly counsel. I just couldn't find answers that made any sense, and the promise of peace that passes all understanding seemed impossible for a grieving person like me.

Then one afternoon amidst tears and prayer, I accepted I might never have answers regarding the loss of my best friend. When I stopped my frantic searching for the whys, it freed me up to take my grief before the Lord and rest in His presence.

As I remained still, that seemingly ever illusive but promised peace that passes all understanding slowly filled my heart and soul. Resting my grief-filled heart in His presence didn't eradicate the pain and grief. Rather, it allowed me the opportunity to recall the above Scripture I committed to memory years ago.

As I reflected on this, I was reminded that His peace isn't found in circumstances or even our ability to understand the whys of life in a fallen world. Our peace is found solely in Him.

Further, we can also encourage our heavy hearts by remembering that He overcame the world by His victory on the cross. Life in this fallen world will not last forever. Neither will our trials and suffering.

While it is healthy to acknowledge and process grief, we cannot allow sorrow to swallow the peace He promises. If your life is riddled with grief today, ask Him to heal your broken heart. Take Him up on His promise of peace by remaining in Him and remembering that He has overcome the world.

None of us are exempt from trials and sorrow, but the promise of peace is for all who will obey His Word by remaining in Him.

Day 67

Resting in the Rock

Jennifer Slattery

"I love You, O Lord, my strength. The Lord is my rock
and my fortress and my deliverer, My God, my rock,
in whom I take refuge; My shield and the horn of my
salvation, my stronghold."

(Psalm 18:1-2 NASB)

In 2006, my husband stepped into an ugly power struggle that
nearly cost him his job. Dishonest and unethical practices had
trickled down from the former boss, infecting all the staff. As a
result, when my husband Steve continually made the right, hard
choice, evil, power-hungry men slandered and attacked him.

The union rep made it his mission to get my Steve fired, which included sending a letter to the CEO telling him how "terrible" Steve
was. Then he printed and prominently displayed the slanderous
letter at the shop.

With every attack against Steve, my anxiety climbed. What if the
union rep succeeded and his company let him go? Where would
he work? How would we pay our bills? What if we lost our home?

Our world felt out of control, and our security felt only as sure as my husband's next paycheck. But then we remembered our sure foundation, the immovable rock upon which we stood.

Psalm 18:1-2 (NASB) says, "I love You, O Lord, my strength. The Lord is my rock, my fortress, and my deliver."

This was written by ancient Israel's second king, a mighty warrior who'd single-handedly defeated a tyrannical giant. Yet, this warrior found strength not in himself and his military prowess, but in his sovereign, all-powerful God. No matter how strong or skilled in battle, apart from God he was vulnerable and insufficient. In the crags of God's love, however, he was amply protected, untouchable.

Towering rocks or bluffs dotted the landscape of ancient Palestine, providing places of refuge, of protection, for all who scampered to them. These elevated geological edifices were difficult to reach and offered shelter within their caverns. Therefore, they became places of safety in times of danger.

Fortresses offered similar protection. The people built heavily fortified cities high upon a cliff where they could see their enemies' approach for miles. Then, they erected stone towers at the highest point in the city.

Can you sense the layers of protection revealed in the Psalm 18 passage? In Christ, we stand high upon an immovable rock of power and grace, further hidden within the clefts of His love. His strength is greater than anything or anyone that comes against us. We are triply protected within His steadfast embrace. He is our sure and constant deliverer, the rock beneath our feet, and the fortress surrounding us.

In 2006, as attacks continued to barrage my husband and our family, we hid ourselves deeply in God. When anxiety arose, we reminded ourselves of where our true security lay, and all we knew to be true about God. He was faithful, loving, and attentive—unconquerable. He was our ever-present provider, the only One with the power to sustain us.

That year, He proved Himself to be all those things and more.

I'm confident He'll do the same for you. Whatever you're facing, whatever is coming against you, rest in this: God's got you. He's standing beside you, within you, and is camped around you. He is your refuge, your rock, and your strong, fortified tower.

You don't have to be strong or know all the answers—that secret that will somehow whisk you to safety—because in Christ, you're already safe.

Day 68

Who Wants to be Disciplined, Anyway?

Carol McCracken

"No discipline seems pleasant at the time, but painful. Later on, however, it produces a harvest of righteousness and peace for those who have been trained by it."

(Hebrews 12:11 NIV)

He did it. My son was graduating from high school. He was in a cap and gown and everything! As he headed up the steps to receive his diploma, he turned around and smiled at me. That was worth more than anything anyone could ever have given me.

There hadn't been peace in our home for quite some time. For seven years after my husband's open-heart surgery, our home life was like walking on eggshells. Waiting for the other shoe to drop.

My son had been diagnosed with Asperger's Syndrome along with a mood disorder. When puberty hit, his chemicals went haywire, and we were challenged with some dark times. With the help of a great doctor along with much prayer, my son finally figured out what was happening and how to manage it.

My husband was facing his mortality, as a congenital heart defect began demanding attention. Three times he almost died. His heart would go out of rhythm, and we'd rush to the emergency room.

Unfortunately, those challenges didn't bring us together. Fear crept in, stealing our peace. We began drawing apart as my husband and I disagreed on how we should handle our son's issues. The tension in our home was tangible.

Looking back, I can now see we were all grappling for some peace in our own way. I was going through the motions as I went to church and led Bible study. But in the interest of "keeping it all together," I wasn't sharing my challenges with anyone. That's not authentic ministry. How could I effectively minister to others when I was navigating this unexpected life all on my own? The internal conflict further drained my peace.

God allowed me to get to the end of myself so He could discipline as a father. We are part of a family of believers, beyond our family of origin. The Bible teaches if we are left without discipline, in which all have participated, then we are illegitimate children and not sons. "The Lord disciplines the one he loves and chastises every son whom he receives" (Hebrews 12:8, 12:6 ESV).

Surrendering my marriage, home and son to Him was painful discipline. When I finally prayed to Him that this was all too much, He now had my attention. I was ready to hear Him. God lovingly worked on me, developing maturity in me, teaching me to do things His way.

In the end of that process, He left me with the gift of my son. Our home life had become steadier. We began trusting in the peace we had found as we allowed God's guidance. My son could focus and graduate.

My inward focus turned outward as I confessed my challenges to my Bible study group. No one had talked openly about issues like mine. I became aware of other women who were also struggling. Women were searching for peace, sometimes like me, by looking in all the wrong places. What God was doing in me began yielding a harvest of righteousness and peace that I could share.

We can know God wants to train us in handling life, because He loves us like a father. Training is discipline, not punishment. Jesus already suffered the punishment for all of our sins. I found that God our Father disciplines His children when we try to handle things on our own, stealing burdens that aren't fully ours to bear. Discipline has its purpose. Ultimately, He wants you, as His child He loves, to find your peace in Him.

Day 69

The Great Escape

Cheri Cowell

"Any temptation you face will be nothing new. But God
is faithful, and He will not let you be tempted beyond
what you can handle. But He always provides a way
of escape so that you will be able to endure and keep
moving forward."

(1 Corinthians 10:13 The Voice)

On a moonless night in 1944, seventy-six POW's escaped through
a thirty-foot tunnel dug by 250 prisoners from the German Stalag
Luft III prison. It would come to be known as *The Great Escape*. All
but three men were recaptured and either killed or tortured. Still,
it stands today as one of history's most daring and brilliant escapes.
In 1963, Steve McQueen starred in the movie that memorialized
this great feat.

Yet, as daring and heroic as this story is, God has devised an escape
plan that is even more amazing. His plan is cunning, because the
tools of your escape—God's Word and His presence—are smug-
gled to us right under Satan's nose. With the use of these tools, we
can endure and keep moving forward out of the prison in which
Satan has us locked toward a life of freedom and peace.

In his letter to the Corinthians, Paul is warning believers about the subtle temptation of idolatry. Most of us aren't worshipping a graven object, but we are tempted to trust in our feelings, our talents, our careers, and our families instead of God. Placing anything or anyone on the throne of our hearts: that is idolatry. God has provided the greatest escape from that temptation ever conceived; reading His Word and walking in His presence will always remind us whom we need to trust.

Tucked within the above Scripture is a phrase that is often quoted out of context and used to make those who fall into temptation feel like failures. The misquote goes something like this—*God won't send you anything you cannot bear.* But in considering the context of this sentence, we see Paul is teaching that temptation is common to us all. God is faithful to stand with us and help us endure until He provides a perfect escape plan when the time is right.

Sometimes the escape is simply a new way to look at things, sometimes it is joy in the midst of the trial, and other times the escape is truly a way out. God's Word and His presence are the most daring and cunning tools of escape ever devised, and they are in your hands every day. Will you make use of those tools today?

Prayer: *I am grateful for Your escape plan that will free me to be at peace with You. Help me use the tools of Your Word and Your Presence to remind me in You alone I trust.*

Day 70

Precious Gifts

Cindy K. Sproles

The LORD is my shepherd, I lack nothing.

(Psalm 23:1 NIV)

I think I have bloody knees. No, I know I have bloody knees. It's the second time I've boogered them up. That time I made a nice dive to catch a runaway cart when we helped our friends move. It was definitely a sight. Both knees poured blood, but despite my clumsiness, we had a good laugh.

But the bloody knees I have now are scarred and scraped from praying. Things like my husband's cancer forced our prayer lives further than usual. As we walked that path, I found that seeking the joy was hard. I also saw my inclination was to pray first for ourselves, before others. We are human after all.

Still, I did my best to continue talking out loud to God in the car, in the house, and in the yard. I have found when I spend my time in prayer for others, then God has space to work in me.

Then, of course, there's timing. His time is certainly not the same as mine. I want a fast answer. Fix it. After all, You're God. Snap Your fingers and fix this! In my imagination, I can see His sweet hand go up, giving me the "wait" sign. Refocus. Regroup. Get back to the real the servanthood of praying for others. Make that necessary room for God to be God.

In the beginning, months were spent simply waiting. That was practice for what was to come—God knew my weakness is waiting. We've learned ... I've learned ... that God places folks around us who want to help us while we wait. It might be through their prayers, a meal, a text, a call...there are tons of ways. The fact is clear, many want to wait with us through the storm.

People like dear friends who, if I didn't call immediately after a doctor's appointment, were calling me. Guiding me. Praying for me. Another wonderful friend, upon hearing about Tim's cancer, sobbed out loud on the phone as he prayed in that instant for us. That is called sharing the burden. Feeling the burden. Some insisted on standing alongside my boys and me during the life-saving surgery that could just as easily taken him.

It was tempting to feel like I was a burden, but who am I to look God in the face and say, "I don't want the help You sent?" So I swallowed my pride and gratefully received each blessing. When I look back at their help, I see the support and help were precious gifts He sent to us.

Recently, I missed a call from Tim's doctor while on the phone with the Ostomy nurse. We were waiting for the final pathology report. We called the doctor's office back, but the call back number went to voice mail. The office was closed. We'd missed talking to the doctor because he makes his calls after office hours. Here we were again ... waiting.

God knows what is best for us, and He guides us by that amazing love. He insisted we wait again. So we waited.

The next morning, the doctor's nurse returned my call.

"Dr. Payne is here, and he wanted me to call you. He didn't want you to wait any longer. Tim's pathology report came back clear. There are no signs of cancer. No malignancy." We both burst into

234

tears. The path to becoming cancer-free had been a permanent, radical surgery that forever changed Tim's daily life, with no real guarantee.

We are grateful for every call, every card, every act of kindness that others shared. Each one was a precious gift given by those who loved us but was orchestrated by Jehovah Jireh, the God who provides.

God proves His love for us daily. We need only to accept it. Jesus called Himself the Good Shepherd Who lays down His life for His sheep (John 10:14-15); the great Shepherd who leaves the ninety-nine to find the one—a vital part of our relationship with Him we so easily forget (Luke 15:4-7). We, as the one, are just as important to God as the rest.

Today we celebrate the waiting and provision that has not only refined us but cleansed us. The result was good, and the waiting was over. Tim had beaten the odds. To say we are blessed is an understatement—and we owe everything to the precious love and care from our heavenly Father, our Shepherd, and we have lacked nothing.

Day 71

Put Peace into Practice

Saundra Dalton-Smith

"Whatever you have learned or received or heard from
me, or seen in me—put it into practice. And the God of
peace will be with you."

(Philippians 4:9 NIV)

Peace does not come naturally to me.

I have always been a good student. I was the kid in elementary
school who had no interest in recess. Given a choice between a
game of kickball or sitting in a quiet corner with a book, and the
book would win every time. I loved reading, and studying came
naturally to me.

When something comes naturally to you, it doesn't require significant effort. It is a part of your natural make-up. It fits your unique
gifts, talents, and personality traits.

But what do you do when something you desperately need does
not come naturally to you?

Daily, I need peace. In a world full of chaos, violence, disappointment, pain, and sorrow, peace is a necessity. Peace is the anchor

in the storms of life, a refuge for the weary. I can recall many days when I failed to find the peace I needed.

I would read books about creating a peaceful setting in my home, but peace was not found in fluffy cushions and lovely artwork. I worshipped my way into peace, but those moments of calm did not last long past the final note sung. I focused on putting peace into practice rather than communing with the God of peace.

It is one thing to feel the peace of God on the inside. It is a far greater thing to know the God of peace is with you. His presence allows you to experience peace in your day-to-day interactions. This peace is one that does not ebb and flow like the tides of the seas. This peace is one that finds a dwelling place to reside.

Throughout Scripture, we learn about men and women of faith believing God for promises beyond anything they could dream or imagine. We receive guidance on how to live a God-honoring life. We hear stories of victory over giants, seas parting for safe passage into freedom, and walls falling as shouts of praise arise to heaven. And we see God do the impossible in the lives of ordinary people. All accomplished with a level of peace that surpasses our ability to understand.

In Philippians 4:9 (NIV), Paul reminds us to put into practice all we know about who God is and what He can do in and through us. He then gives us a promise with the power to silence every fear and quiet every doubt: "…and the God of peace will be with you."

In his final appeal to believers, Paul challenges us to change how we view peace. Although often seen as a human feeling, turning to God transforms peace into something (or rather someone) far more excellent.

I may fail at being able to create the peace I desire, but God never fails. He never leaves me nor forsakes me. He remains faithful through it all.

Peace does not have to come naturally to me, because the Holy Spirit in me will bring it about as I practice fellowship with Him. After all, peace is a fruit of the Spirit (Galatians 5:22).

Day 72

Word of the Year

Cynthia Ruchti

"He that dwelleth in the secret place of the most High shall abide under the shadow of the Almighty"

(Psalm 91:1 KJV).

My search for a word-of-the-year to ponder and consider—a God-honoring word—stumped me one January. God's Word is full of excellent choices—grace, courage, mercy, strength, forgiveness, joy, boldness, humility ... But I'd used them all, as if concepts like those could ever be exhausted.

If I'm convinced of anything, it's that after decades of loving and serving Him, He's not done shaping me, crafting me, honing the rough edges. So, it was important for me to train my spirit to "listen" for that word-of-the-year and spend 365 days lingering with it. Ooh! Linger. That would have been a good one.

Instead, deep inside I sensed He wanted me to dig into a phrase rather than a word—If I dwell. Even without looking it up, I knew that wasn't a complete sentence. Three words, Lord? And my year-long focus starts with "If"?

I almost dismissed it as my imagination rather than His prompting. I'm glad I didn't. It's been life-altering.

What are the end results if I dwell in any other place than in the shadow of the Almighty God?

If I dwell in past hurts …

If I dwell in resentment or bitterness …

If I dwell on that unkind word my husband said …

If I dwell on what I don't and can't have …

If I dwell on the losses of the previous year …

If I dwell on accomplishments rather than serving …

If I dwell on what I know from childhood rather than continually growing in my faith …

If I dwell on the chaos that rages in the world around me …

… then I am toast. I'm wrecked, broken, weighed down, encumbered, forgetful of God's mercies and forgiveness, discontented, disappointed, stuck, misaligned, vulnerable, miserable, and missing it.

If I set up camp in the cesspool of bitterness, it won't be long before my whole being stinks. If I plant my tent stakes in the hard soil of rehashing my past mistakes, attempting to make a home in what God has already erased in His endless mercy, the canvas over me will collapse on constant fitful, sleepless nights. If I pull my caravan into an area where anger swarms like wasps and floodwaters of self-interest or self-aggrandizement continue to rise, I'll soon find myself stung beyond recognition and floating on what destroys, not what can save.

But if…

If I choose daily, hourly, to dwell in the secret place of the Most High God, the shadow over me is His protective shade. The walls around me aren't confining, but His ever-safe embrace. The surround-sound will be His steady heartbeat. The voice in my ear will never lie to me or condemn me. Dwelling in His shadow is the ultimate definition of peace.

Proverbs 1:33 (CEB) reminds me that my obedience to God, my responsiveness to Him is the gateway into that shelter. "Those who obey me," God says, "will dwell securely, untroubled by the dread of harm." Security. Peace. Freedom from dread or anxiety. And cocooned in the tender embrace of the One who can even oust worry about harm.

It's His invitation, His welcome mat, but it's my choice where I dwell. If peace is what I crave, could the decision be any more obvious?

Alphabetical Index of Authors

Debbie Alsdorf has been a women's ministry leader for over 30 years. She is an author, speaker, mentor, certified life coach, and the founder of Design4Living Ministries. Debbie is the author of twelve books. She and her husband Ray live in California with two crazy but very loved little dogs. Learn more at debbiealsdorf.com

Nan Corbitt Allen has written over 100 published dramatic musicals, sketchbooks, and collections. A three-time Dove Award winner, Nan's works have been performed around the world. Nan teaches English and Creative Writing at Truett McConnell University. Visit nancorbittallen.com.

Lori Altebaumer loves sharing the joys of living a Christ-centered life. She enjoys traveling and visiting her adult children, where she can rummage through their refrigerators and food pantries while complaining there's nothing here good to eat. (Payback!) Visit lorialtebaumer.com.

Candy Arrington has written hundreds of articles and devotionals, often on tough topics. She is a native South Carolinian, who gains writing inspiration from historic architecture, vintage photographs, nature, and the application of Biblical principles to everyday life. Visit CandyArrington.com.

Dianne Barker is a conference speaker, radio host, and author of eleven books including the bestselling *Twice Pardoned* and award-winning *I Don't Chase the Garbage Truck Down the Street in My Bathrobe Anymore! Organizing for the Maximum Life.* Visit diannebarker.com.

Janet Chester Bly has been writing since 1981 to prepare readers to receive God's truth. Bly Books contain grit and grace, humor, and inspiration. Her fiction and nonfiction books contain entertaining tales and practical tips with a western country flair. Visit blybooks.com.

Crystal Bowman is a bestselling, award-winning author of more than 100 books, including *Mothers In Waiting—Healing and Hope for Those with Empty Arms.* She and her husband have three married children and seven huggable grandchildren. You can find more on Crystal at crystalbowman.com.

Kristine Brown is a communicator at heart, sharing insight with her readers in relatable ways. Her lessons highlight God's powerful Word and redemptive grace. She is the author of the book, *Over It. Conquering Comparison to Live Out God's Plan.*
Check out kristinebrown.net.

Dianne Butts has written 300+ articles for Christian magazines, six books, and has contributed to twenty more books, including *Chicken Soup for the Soul.* She and her husband are members of the Christian Motorcyclists Association. Visit DianneEButts.com or her blog at ButtsAboutWriting.blogspot.com.

Pamela Christian is an international itinerant minister and Bible teacher She hosts her own internet television show, *Faith to Live By.* She holds a certificate in Apologetics from Biola. Her passion is to help others discover the life-giving truth she's been blessed to find. PamelaChristianMinistries.com.

Julie Zine Coleman helps others understand and know an unexpected God. She has an M.A. in biblical studies and is the managing editor for *Arise Daily.* She is the author of *Unexpected Love: God's Heart Revealed through Jesus' Conversations with Women.* Visit her at unexpectedgod.com.

Debora Coty is a speaker, columnist, and award-winning author of over 40 inspirational books, including the bestselling *Too Blessed to be Stressed* series. She lives in central Florida with her long-suffering husband. Find more on Debora at DeboraCoty.com.

Cheri Cowell is the author of *365 Devotions for Peace.* As an author and sidewalk theologian, Cheri writes and speaks from a refreshing vulnerability about her own struggles with the deep questions of faith. She is a graduate of Asbury Theological Seminary. Find out more at chericowell.com.

Peggy Cunningham and her husband are missionaries in Bolivia. In 1999, they founded Rumi Rancho Ministries to work with the Quechua people and have a children's ministry there. *Shape Your Soul* is her latest devotional book for women. Visit PeggyCuningham.org.

Saundra Dalton-Smith is a physician, author, and speaker helping women heal in their body, mind, and spirit. Her books include *Set Free to Live Free: Breaking Through the 7 Lies Women Tell Themselves* and *Come Empty: Pour Out Life's Hurts and Receive God's Healing Love*. Visit IChooseMyBestLife.com.

Deb DeArmond is an expert in the fields of relationship and conflict resolution. A writer and speaker, she focuses on family and women. Her books include *Don't Go to Bed Angry: Stay Up and Fight*. Read Deb at her website, *Family Matters, at* debdearmond.com.

Lilian de Silva is the founder of "Moratuwa Fellowship of Christian Women." She has published three books, including *Be an Overcomer: Jesus' Letters to the Seven Churches*, and a worship music album. The productions she has composed have appeared on national television.

Janet Eckles. Blindness tried to darken her life, but Janet became an international speaker, best-selling author, personal success coach, and radio host. Her books include *Contagious Courage: A Thirty Day Journey to Overcoming Stress and Anxiety*. Visit janetperezeckles.com.

Lynn Eib is a long-time cancer survivor, a patient advocate, and an award-winning journalist. She has six titles with Tyndale House Publishing, including *When God & Cancer Meet*. Find free resources for cancer patients and their caregivers at lynneib.com.

Natalie Flake Ford teaches at Truett McConnell University. She is also a licensed professional counselor. Natalie speaks at numerous conferences and churches each year about how God has turned her tears to joy. Learn more at tearstojoy.org.

Grace Fox is a career global worker and the author of ten books.

She's a regular contributor to *Mornings with Jesus* (Guideposts) and a member of the First 5 writing team (P31 Ministries). She and her husband of 39 years live on a sailboat near Vancouver, British Columbia. Learn more about Grace at gracefox.com.

Karen DeArmond Gardner is a 30-year survivor of domestic violence. She has spent 15 years helping others find freedom, restoration, and redemption. Karen serves on the Board of Directors for Arukah House, a home for women coming out of sex trafficking and abuse. Visit crackthesilence.com.

Nancy Kay Grace is captivated by God's grace and loves to share about embracing it in everyday life. Nancy and her husband, Rick, serve the Lord in Arkansas, where he is a senior pastor. Her book, *The Grace Impact,* was the 2016 Next Generation Indie Book of the Year. Visit nancykaygrace.com.

Debb Hackett has been a writer, broadcaster, speaker, and radio journalist for more than twenty years. Married to a test pilot, Debb writes for military wives and lives just outside Washington D.C. with her husband and children. She blogs at debbhackett.com

Vicki Heath is the National Director of the faith-based wellness ministry, First Place 4 Health. Vicki is an author and nationally-known speaker. She holds certifications with American Council on Exercise and Body & soul Fitness. Vicki is a pastor's wife and she and her husband, Rob, have four grown children and six grandchildren. Learn more at firstplaceforhealth.com

Elaine Helms encourages audiences and readers to live the abundant life Jesus came to give us. Prayer Coordinator for My Hope America with Billy Graham. Her book, *Prayer 101, What Every Intercessor Needs to Know* re-released in August 2019. Visit ChurchPrayerMinistries.org.

Cheryl Hollar is a contributing writer at mytakeontv.com. Her book, *A Fans' Guide to Hawaii Five-O* takes a first-ever look behind the camera with directors and writers of the original and reboot *Hawaii Five-0*. She is a member of Franklinton Baptist Church in Franklinton, NC.

Doris Hoover lives in Florida, but she also spends time along the coast of Maine. Her passion is discovering God's messages in nature and sharing them with others. You can visit Doris at captivatedbythecreator.com.

Kathy Howard has a passion for God's Word that's contagious. She has taught the Bible in dozens of states, internationally, and in a wide range of venues. Kathy is the author of eight books and five Bible studies, including *Lavish Grace*. She provides free discipleship resources and blogs at KathyHoward.org.

Donna Jones is a national speaker and pastor's wife and has spoken across the U.S. and on four continents. She's the author of *Seek: A Woman's Guide to Meeting God* and several Bible studies. Donna's a sucker for strong coffee and cute shoes. Connect with Donna at donnajones.org.

Louise Tucker Jones is a speaker, columnist, and author of four books. Her poignant life stories have been published in hundreds of magazines and anthologies. Louise coauthored the award-winning book, *Extraordinary Kids*. For more, visit LouiseTuckerJones.com.

Lane Jordan is a best-selling author and an international inspirational speaker. She encourages, supports, and motivates women to organize their lives and time. Read her blogs at LaneJordanMinistries.com and PathwaysToOrganization.com.

Rebecca Barlow Jordan loves to paint encouragement on the hearts of others. She has authored and contributed to over 20 books and written over 2000 articles and other inspirational pieces. Find Rebecca and her encouraging blog at www.rebeccabarlowjordan.com.

Carol Kent is a bestselling author and international speaker. She's the executive director of the Speak Up Conference, a ministry committed to helping Christians develop their speaking and writing skills. She's authored more than 25 books and Bible studies, including *Becoming a Woman of Influence*. See more at CarolKent. org and SpeakUpConference.com

Michelle Lazurek is an award-winning author, national speaker, pastor's wife, and mother. She loves to help people encounter God and engage with the world around them. When not writing, you can find her enjoying a Starbucks latte and collecting vintage records. Visit michellelazurek.com.

Carole Lewis is Director Emeritus of First Place for Health. A warm, transparent and humorous communicator, Carole speaks at conferences around the country. She is also the author of fifteen popular books. Carole lives in Houston, Texas, and was widowed in 2014. She has three adult children (one deceased), eight grandchildren, and 8 great-grandchildren.

Lee Ann Mancini is an adjunct professor at South Florida Bible College and Theological Seminary. She is the author of the *Sea Kids* book series and an executive producer of the new *Sea Kids* animation series. Find out more at leeannmancini.com.

Babbie Mason is a two-time Dove Award winning singer-songwriter and a best-selling author and speaker. Her ministry has blessed millions around the globe for more than three decades. She was inducted into the Christian Music Hall of Fame and has been nominated for eleven Dove Awards and received nominations for the Grammy, the Emmy, and the Stellar Awards. She and her husband Charles live on a farm in Georgia. See more at babbie.com

Dianne Neal Matthews is the author of four daily devotional books including *The One Year Women of the Bible* and *Designed for Devotion: A 365-Day Journey from Genesis to Revelation* (Selah Award winner). You can learn more at DianneNealMatthews.com.

Deborah McCormick Maxey is an award-winning writer. Her first novel, *The Endling*, published by Firefly Southern Fiction, Lighthouse Publishing of the Carolinas, will be released soon. Along with a love for storytelling, Deborah is worship leader at her church, a devoted wife, mother, grandmother, and a licensed therapist in her counseling center in Lynchburg Virginia.

Carol McCracken has been a Bible teacher for over twenty years and serves the Leadership Development and Women's ministry at her church. Her passion is to make the Bible come alive for women to enhance a real relationship with Jesus. She contributes to ChristianDevotions.us.

Lucinda Secrest McDowell is a storyteller and seasoned mentor who engages both heart and mind. A graduate of Gordon-Conwell Theological Seminary and Furman University, McDowell is the author of 15 books, including *Life-Giving Choices* and *Soul Strong*. She blogs at encouragingwords.net.

Heidi McLaughlin is an international speaker and author. She is a mom and step mom of a wonderful, eclectic blended family of 5 children and 12 grandchildren. She has been widowed twice. Her latest book is *Restless for More: Fulfillment in Unexpected Places*. Visit heidimclaughlin.com.

Cindi McMenamin is an award-winning writer and national speaker who helps women and couples strengthen their relationship with God and others. She has authored 17 books including *Drama Free: Finding Peace When Emotions Overwhelm You*. Visit Strength-ForTheSoul.com.

Gari Meacham loves words. Spoken, unspoken, written, recited, or sung. Mostly, she loves God's words—the Bible. She is an author, speaker, baseball wife, and nonprofit CEO. Her highly acclaimed books, workbooks, and DVDs include *Spirit Hunger* and *Truly Fed*. She and her baseball man, major league coach Bobby Meacham, live in Houston, Texas. Learn more at garimeacham.com.

Edie Melson Find your voice, live your story ... is the foundation of Edie's message, whether she's addressing parents, military families, readers of fiction, or writers. An author, blogger, and speaker, she's encouraged audiences around the world. Connect with her further at EdieMelson.com.

Kathy Collard Miller is the author of over 55 books, including the *Daughters of the King* Bible study series. She has encouraged audiences in 35 states and 8 foreign countries. Visit her at Kathy-CollardMiller.com.

Donna Nabors is a wife, mom, and grandma focused on filling her spiritual jewelry box. Through disappointments in life, she shares that the treasures from God's Word are where we find the strength to stand. Donna's hobbies include antique shopping and organizing. Visit donnanabors.com.

Ava Pennington is an author, Bible Study Fellowship (BSF) teacher, and speaker. Her most recent book, *Daily Reflections on the Names of God*, is endorsed by Kay Arthur of Precepts Ministries. Ava has also published stories in 30+ anthologies. Visit AvaWrites.com.

Karen Porter is a speaker, author, entrepreneur, and a successful businesswoman. She is the author of seven books, including *If You Give a Girl A Giant* and *Amplify!* She is the founder of kae Creative Solutions and the co-owner of Bold Vision Books, a traditional publishing company. Learn more at karenporter.com

Anita Renfroe has performed at The Grand Ole Opry and appeared on "Good Morning America," "Dr.Phil," "Oprah and Friends," "The Early Show," "Fox and Friends," "Huckabee," and many more. Anita routinely packs venues with her comedy concerts and inspirational women's conferences. She and her husband John live in Wichita, KS with their spoiled dogs. Learn more at anitarenfroe.com

Rhonda Rhea is a TV personality for Christian Television Network and an award-winning humor columnist. She is the author of 19 books, including the *Messy to Meaningful* books and the hilarious novels, *Off-Script and Over-Caffeinated* and *Turtles in the Road*. You can find her at RhondaRhea.com.

Lori Roeleveld is an author and speaker who enjoys making comfortable Christians late for dinner. She's authored four encouraging, unsettling books. Her latest release is *The Art of Hard Conversations: Biblical Tools for the Tough Talks that Matter*. She speaks her mind at loriroeleveld.com.

Linda Rooks has ministry of hope for those in broken marriages. Her award-winning books walk with those in the midst of marital breakdown to bring hope and practical guidance to those desiring reconciliation. Linda's articles have appeared in numerous publications. Visit LindaRooks.com.

Christina Rose is an author, trainer, and speaker. A devoted mom of two daughters, Christina loves spending time in nature and hosting gatherings for family and friends. She is a Daughter of the American Revolution (DAR) whose ancestors fought in the Revolutionary War. Visit christinarose.org.

Cynthia Ruchti tells stories hemmed in Hope. Her more than 30 novels and nonfiction books have been awarded a number of retailer, reviewer, reader, and other industry awards. She and her husband live in the heart of Wisconsin, not far from their three children and six grandchildren. You can find her and her books at cynthiaruchti.com.

Fran Sandin is a retired nurse, wife, mother, and grandmother in Greenville, Texas. She enjoys baking, flower arranging, hiking, and traveling with her husband, Jim. Fran is the author of *See You Later, Jeffrey,* and *Touching the Clouds: True Stories to Strengthen Your Faith*. Visit fransandin.com.

Jill Savage is the author of 14 books, two co-authored with her husband Mark. Reading any of their books is like sitting down for a cup of coffee with a friend. Honest, hope-filled, practical with just the right amount of humor, you'll find yourself reaching for another! See more at jillsavage.org

Sheri Schofield is an award-winning children's author-illustrator and children's ministry veteran of 40 years. Sheri was named Writer of the Year in 2018 at the Colorado Christian Writers' Conference for her work in sharing the gospel of Jesus. You can follow her ministry for kids at sherischofield.com.

Georgia Shaffer knows what it's like to bounce back after repeated challenges and find God's peace. As an author, professional certified coach and licensed psychologist in PA, she offers individual and group coaching. She is also the author of five books, including *A Gift of Mourning Glories: Restoring Your Life after Loss.* Connect with Georgia at GeorgiaShaffer.com.

Linda Evans Shepherd is the president of Right to the Heart Ministries and the CEO of the Advanced Writers and Speakers Association (AWSA). She publishes *Arise Daily* and *Leading Hearts* magazine and is an award-winning speaker and author who has written numerous books. Visit gottopray.com.

Monica Schmelter is the General Manager for WHTN (Christian Television Network) and host of the television program *Bridges*. Monica's book, *Messy to Meaningful,* will help you sort out the unnecessary spiritual things weighing you down. Visit monicascmelter.com.

Jennifer Slattery is a writer and speaker who's addressed women's groups across the nation. She loves to help women discover and live out who they are in Christ. She's the author of *Hometown Healing* and numerous other titles and maintains a devotional blog at JenniferSlatteryLivesOutLoud.com.

Cindy K. Sproles is the co-founder of Christian Devotions Ministries. She is a best-selling author and a speaker for writers and women's conferences across the country. Her two latest books are *Liar's Winter* and *What Mama Left Behind.* Learn more at cindysproles. com.

Sharon Tedford is a British storyteller who uses her gifts as a worship leader, author, and speaker to connect with her listeners, inviting them into a revitalized relationship with God. She is mother to three teenagers and the wife of an Irishman. You can connect with her at 61-things.com.

Sheryl Giesbrecht Turner's focus is on exchanging hurt for hope—a message she shares as a radio and television personality, author, and speaker. Hundreds of her columns, magazine, and devotional articles have appeared in *Focus on The Family Magazine* and many others. Visit sherylgiesbrecht.com.

Peggy Sue Wells History buff and island votary, Peggy Sue is an international speaker and the best-selling author of 29 books including *Chasing Sunrise, Homeless for the Holidays,* and *Best Decisions a Single Parent Can Make.* Find out more at peggysuewells.com.

Lori Wildenberg is a national speaker, parent-family educator, and author of 5 parenting books including *Messy Journey: How Grace and Truth Offer the Prodigal a Way Home.* Go to loriwildenberg.com for more information.

A.C. Williams loves cats, country living, and all things Japanese. She'd rather be barefoot, but if she isn't, her socks will never match. Amy prefers Trixie Belden to Nancy Drew, wears her watch on the wrong wrist, and feels Mr. Darcy is her love language. Follow her on social media @free2bfearless.

Sharon Wilharm is a Christian speaker, women's ministry leader, popular media guest, and award-winning filmmaker. Her heart's desire is to encourage women in their walk with the Lord, showing them how to find God's will for their life through prayer and Scripture. Find out more at sharonwilharm.com.

Debbie Wilson Drawing from her walk with Christ and years as a Christian counselor, coach, and Bible teacher, Debbie helps women enjoy fruitful and grace-filled lives. She is the author of *Little Women, Big God,* and *Give Yourself a Break.* Connect with her at debbieWwilson.com.

Karen Wingate writes and speaks about her journey of discovery after a random surgery doubled her life-long limited eyesight. Author of over 350 magazine articles, compilation stories, devotions, and curriculum guides, Karen blogs at graceonparade.com.

Bible Translations and Versions

Made in the USA
Columbia, SC
02 August 2021